Cambridge Elements ≡

Elements in the Economics of Emerging Markets
edited by
Bruno S. Sergi
Harvard University

PRODUCTIVITY IN EMERGING COUNTRIES

Methodology and Firm-Level Analysis Based on International Enterprise Business Surveys

Alvaro Escribano

University Carlos III of Madrid

Jorge Pena

IE University

CAMBRIDGE
UNIVERSITY PRESS

CAMBRIDGE
UNIVERSITY PRESS

University Printing House, Cambridge CB2 8BS, United Kingdom

One Liberty Plaza, 20th Floor, New York, NY 10006, USA

477 Williamstown Road, Port Melbourne, VIC 3207, Australia

314–321, 3rd Floor, Plot 3, Splendor Forum, Jasola District Centre,
New Delhi – 110025, India

79 Anson Road, #06–04/06, Singapore 079906

Cambridge University Press is part of the University of Cambridge.

It furthers the University's mission by disseminating knowledge in the pursuit of
education, learning, and research at the highest international levels of excellence.

www.cambridge.org
Information on this title: www.cambridge.org/9781108829441
DOI: 10.1017/9781108909938

First published 2021

A catalogue record for this publication is available from the British Library.

ISBN 978-1-108-82944-1 Paperback
ISSN 2631-8598 (online)
ISSN 2631-858X (print)

Cambridge University Press has no responsibility for the persistence or accuracy of
URLs for external or third-party internet websites referred to in this publication
and does not guarantee that any content on such websites is, or will remain,
accurate or appropriate.

Productivity in Emerging Countries

Methodology and Firm-Level Analysis based on International Enterprise Business Surveys

Elements in the Economics of Emerging Markets

DOI:10.1017/9781108909938
First published online: May 2021

Alvaro Escribano
University Carlos III of Madrid

Jorge Pena
IE University

Author for correspondence: Alvaro Escribano, alvaroe@eco.uc3m.es

Abstract: Emerging countries are increasingly concerned with improving their competitiveness and productivity. This Element develops a robust econometric methodology, based on controlling for usual unobservable effects at the firm or plant level. By robust empirical results in total factor productivity (TFP), we mean estimating investment climate (IC) elasticities, or semi-elasticities, with equal signs and similar magnitudes for more than ten different competing TFP measures. The key to achieving similar empirical results for several TFP measures is to avoid having the problem of omitted variables, achieved through imputation of large proportions of missing observations in relevant variables (i.e., the capital stock). Furthermore, through the use of a new concept of aggregate TFP (TFP^{IC}), which measures the associated IC effects on firms' TFP, we are able to make meaningful cross-country firm-level productivity comparisons, avoiding the usual problem of comparing apples with oranges that would otherwise occur if we directly compare country's TFP measurements.

Keywords: total factor productivity (TFP), investment climate (IC), TFP^{IC}, observable fixed eEffects, robust investment climate effects, production functions, input-output elasticities, marginal IC effects on TFP, average IC effects on TFP

JEL Codes: C23, C18, L25, L11, F14, C51

ISBNs: 9781108829441 (PB), 9781108909938 (OC)
ISSNs: 2631-8598 (online), 2631-858X (print)

Contents

1 Introduction   1

2 Econometric Productivity Methodologies at the
Firm Level   11

3 Enterprise Surveys and Imputation of Missing
Observations   23

4 Empirical Results on the Impact of IC Variables on TFP in
Turkey   27

5 Evidence of the Robustness of TFP Measures and of the
Empirical Results of the Effects of the IC   63

6 International Countries' Investment Climate Assessments
Based on Enterprise Business Surveys of Other Selected
Emerging Countries and Regions   71

7 Conclusions and Further Extensions   76

Appendix A: Productivity in Levels (or Logs) versus
Productivity in Differences (or Rates of Growth)   79

Appendix B: Stata Do-File that Replicates the Results   85

References   99

1 Introduction

Emerging countries are focusing on issues of competitiveness and total factor productivity (TFP) improvements through microeconomic reform programs. As countries face the pressures and effects of globalization, they are looking for ways to stimulate growth and employment in this context of increased openness. From Southeast Asia to Latin America, countries are reformulating their strategies and making competitiveness/productivity enhancement a key priority on government agendas.

In order to understand large international income differences, it is necessary to explain productivity (TFP) differences, as noted by Prescott (1998), whose main candidates for explaining these differences are resistance to the adoption of new technologies and to the efficient use of current operating technologies, which in turn are conditioned by institutional and policy issues. Cole et al. (2004) have also argued that Latin America has not replicated the economic success of the West because of the productivity (TFP) gap. They point out that competitive barriers are the promising channels for understanding the low productivity observed in Latin American countries. It is now accepted, both conceptually and empirically, that the scope and nature of regulations on economic activity and factor markets – the so-called investment climate and business environment – can significantly and often adversely influence productivity, growth and economic activity.[1] An important component of a country's competitiveness is the existence of a *good investment climate or an appropriate business environment*.

For example, the Organization for Economic Cooperation and Development (OECD) identifies as productivity drivers those coming from technical change, economies of scale, efficiency change or rate of capacity utilization. Others, such as the Bureau of Labor Statistics (BLS) add reallocation of resources. Denison (1962, 1974) add other drivers of productivity such as improvements in resources allocation, increases in knowledge or eliminations of restrictions to the efficient use of resources. Grifell-Tajé and Lovel (2015) grouped the productivity drivers as internal factors that depend on the quality of the management (human resources, managerial practices, reallocation across division and product lines, adoption of new technologies, etc.) and external factors or those beyond the control of the managers (institutions, ownership, competitive environment, regulation, structural reforms, liberalization, public R&D, demographics, etc.).

---

[1] See McMillan, 1998 and 2004; OECD, 2001a and b; Wilkinson, 2001; Alexander, Bell and Knowles, 2004; Rodrik and Subramanian, 2004.

The investment climate (IC), as defined in the World Development Report, World Bank (2005), is "the set of locally specific factors that determine opportunities and incentives for firms to invest productively, create jobs and grow": we aim to capture those internal and external drivers by interviewing the managers of the firms (survey data). In this Element, we evaluate the empirical effects of the IC on total factor productivity (TFP) at the plant level, using data from international surveys or enterprise business surveys (ESs) of the World Bank. These surveys are stratified random samples of firms, mainly *manufacturing firms,* with the stratification variables being industry and region, see Table 2 for information on Turkey. The sampling processes are carried out in close collaboration with the regional statistical agencies that provided the necessary information on the total census of manufacturing enterprises in each country,[2] maintaining the basic structure and questions of each IC survey common to all countries. These surveys represent a very rich source of quantitative information at the enterprise level since *these variables are generally considered to be unobservable fixed effects.* In our case, they will allow us to analyze new determinants of the business environment and new sources of possible bottlenecks to business growth.

ESs in most developing countries are unbalanced panels of a large number of firms with two important characteristics: (a) a few (1–3) years of time observations on production function variables at the plant level and (b) a single (1) year of firm-level information on the IC of many firms. However, for the latter, the World Bank-designed ESs only provides one year of data for the production function variables.

In the initial studies Escribano and Guasch (2004, 2005) considered that, unless there are major structural changes in the economy, these plant-level IC values should not change much from the previous two or three consecutive years and therefore they treated that information as observable fixed effects. For example, consider the infrastructure IC variable, named *number of power outages suffered* at a plant level in a given year. Since the infrastructure quality of the electricity system is given in the short term, the expected number of power outages for the company should be similar (fixed effects) for consecutive years.[3]

Hall and Jones (1999) argue that to explain differences in the levels of long-term economic success between countries, one is forced to focus on the most

---

[2] In order to ensure a sufficient number of large establishments in the sample of manufacturing companies, a sampling approach was applied which over represents large enterprises.

[3] J. Levinsohn suggested that we compare our initial recall results with those obtained using only cross-sectional data, without repeating the IC values for previous years. This issue is addressed later on in this Element.

basic determinants, such as infrastructure and the persistent barriers that keep technology and capital from moving rapidly across borders, and they note that "the long-term determinants of economic success are factors that change slowly over time."

In this Element, we focus on the case of Turkey, which is an emerging economy in transition, seeking ways to increase growth and stimulate productivity in order to expand the production possibility frontiers and converge to the income levels of the United States, and other European countries. The lack of convergence in terms of per capita income with respect to China over the last twelve years (2008–20), shown in Figure 1, reveals the surprising weakness of the Turkish economy in terms of competitiveness or in terms of labor productivity. Once Turkey has ensured a reasonable level of macroeconomic stability, in order to achieve the goals of increasing production and reducing unemployment, the main objective of the Turkish economic authorities is to seek ways to stimulate the country's competitiveness and productivity; a good IC is now recognized as one of them.[4] Relative to the United States, Figure 1 shows the stagnation of per capita income with respect to the United States from 1991 to 2008 and the divergence in labor productivity that was reduced from 70 percent of the US figure in 1991 to nearly 62 percent in 2008. After 2009, Turkey started converging in per capita income and labor productivity reaching, in the last case, 80 percent of the US figure in 2020.

A good candidate for explaining the lack of convergence in labor productivity in Turkey is the ability of the economy to produce more output with the same amount of inputs, or improving TFP.[5] Other candidates to explain the labor productivity convergence/divergence are the evolution of the capital-labor ratio, the ability/difficulties of firms to enter and compete successfully in world markets, or the ability/barriers in factor markets to integrate labor supply into the production of goods and services.

---

[4] For example, Kasper (2002) shows that the misunderstood "state paternalism" has generally created unjustified barriers to business activity, resulting in poor growth and a stifling environment. Kerr (2002) shows that the regulatory impasse is a huge deterrent to investment and economic growth. McMillan (1998) argues that obstructive government regulation prior to 1984 was the key issue in New Zealand's decline in global per capita income rankings. de Soto (2002) describes a key adverse effect of heavy business regulation and weak property rights: with costly business regulation, fewer firms choose to register and more become informal. In addition, if registering property entails high transaction costs, assets are less likely to be officially registered and therefore cannot be used as collateral for loans, thus becoming "dead" capital. Similarly, Hidalgo-Cabrillana and Erosa (2008) point out that the ability to enforce contracts affects the allocation of resources among entrepreneurs in different productivities and among industries with different external financing needs.

[5] Differences in labor productivity have traditionally been attributed to differences in TFP in the literature, see Cole et al. (2004).

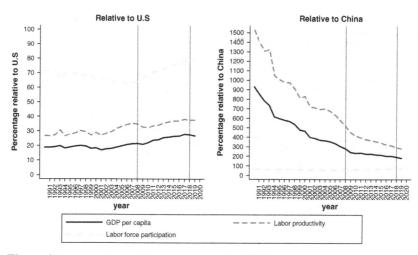

Figure 1 Decomposition of the gap in per capita GDP between Turkey and the United States and China, 1990–2019

Notes: The GDP per capita (Y/P) is decomposed into labor productivity (Y/L) and employment-to-population ratio (L/P) using the following expression: $(Y/P) = (Y/L)*(L/P)$; The expression relative to the United States (US) becomes $[(Y^{TUR}/P^{TUR})/(Y^{US}/P^{US})] = [(Y^{TUR}/L^{TUR})/(Y^{US}/L^{US})]*[(L^{TUR}/P^{TUR})/(L^{US}/P^{US})]$.

Source: Penn World Table Version 6.2, Center for International Comparison of Production, Income and Prices, University of Pennsylvania, September 2006.

The main objective of this Element is to describe the econometric methodology behind many of the research papers written by the Element's authors and their co-authors on the role of the IC determinants and their impact on per capita GDP and labor-productivity as illustrated in Figure 1. The focus of the econometric methodology described in this Element is to use the rich and comprehensive set of plant-level information contained in the IC surveys, or enterprise surveys, of Turkey in order to obtain econometric estimates with robust empirical impacts, while at the same time facing the main difficulties inherent in the poor quality of the databases of emerging countries with many missing observations in key variables such as the capital stock. In particular, we use the ES data from the Turkish case, see Tables 1 and 2, for the years 2012 and 2018 to meet the proposed target. The ES database has become a key tool for both policymakers and researchers in investigating the causes of the traditional dichotomy of poor/rich countries. The strength of this family of surveys is the rich set of information on the quality of physical and social infrastructure provided by business managers.

In addition, this Element aims to compare the IC cross-section results obtained in 2018 and 2012 with those obtained by recall data years ago, but

Table 1 Basic information on the database and the econometric evaluation

Data Base	i. Econometric Regression Models used to identify the main IC effects on TFP		ii. Alternative Evaluations of the main IC Effects
	Dependent variables or variables on the left-hand side of the equation (regression)	Explanatory variables or the right-hand side of the equation (regression)	
Business ES data from The World Bank	Sales and Total Factor Productivity (TFP)	Selection of the marginal effects of 40 IC, business variables + other control variables (industry, region and time)	We present the marginal effects, the average effects and also evaluate the IC effects on aggregate productivity (TFP), as well as their impact on average productivity (TFP) and the allocative efficiency term of the Olley and Pakes (1996) decomposition.

applying a similar methodology to the data of the previous ESs of Turkey, carried out in 2009. The results of the 2009 econometric analysis were the basis of the World Bank document for its Turkey country report of 2007. The description of the initial econometric methodology applied to Turkey and the main results can be found in Escribano et al. (2008b). Table 2 summarizes the list of forty IC variables and variable transformations (in logs, %, etc.) used for the econometrics analysis applied to Turkey 2008 and 2018 in this Element.

The central core of the methodology is a system of equations relating the IC as variables on the right side of the equation (explanatory) and its relationship with the efficiency of firms, represented by the TFP as a dependent variable. Table 2 includes the definitions of the forty IC variables and other control variables used in the estimation. From these forty IC variables, the most relevant/significant variables will be selected. The econometric methodology described in this Element develops, extends and updates the unpublished model specification strategy of Escribano and Guasch (2004 and 2005) and Escribano et al. (2008b).

Once we have identified significant marginal effects (elasticities, etc.) of the IC on the TFP, we evaluate the contributions of each significant IC variable in terms of the Olley and Pakes (1996) decomposition of the aggregate productivity and its two components; the sample mean TFP and the allocative efficiency term as explained in the following (see also Escribano and Guasch 2004, 2005, and Escribano, Guasch and Pena, 2019).[6]

The TFP methodology in this Element was initially developed to explain why different researchers from The World Bank, dealing with common issues on the infrastructure and finance effects on TFP, sometimes reached opposite conclusions (different signs in the coefficients of the key IC variables and different relevant IC variables) even if they were using the same database from ESs of the same countries.[7] For example, for the case of Guatemala, Honduras and Nicaragua, see Escribano and Guasch (2004, 2005).

---

[6] This impact assessment procedure has been applied to many countries, as background econometric work for the so-called Investment Climate Assessments carried out by the World Bank. In the list of countries analyzed with this methodology by A. Escribano and J. Pena and co-authors, include Algeria, Bangladesh, Bangladesh, Bolivia, Botswana, Brazil, Burkina Faso, Cameroon, Chile, Colombia, Costa Rica, Croatia, Ecuador, Egypt, El Salvador, Eritrea, Ethiopia, Guatemala, Honduras, Honduras, India, Indonesia, Kenya, Madagascar, Malawi, Mali, Mauritania, Mauritius, Mexico, Morocco, Namibia, Nicaragua, Niger, Pakistan, Pakistan, Peru, Senegal, South Africa, Swaziland, Tanzania, the Philippines, Turkey, Uganda and Zambia.

[7] In fact, the different researchers were part of different units (infrastructure, finance, etc.) of the World Bank (WB) in Washington, DC. To answer these methodological questions, the WB launched a competitive open call for econometric proposals. Several methodological proposals were suggested. The econometric methodology described in this Element was selected because it was the only one capable of explaining the previous contradictory results, identifying their cause and proposing an alternative general TFP methodology and specification strategy for the IC effects on TFP.

Table 2 Definition of the 40 IC variables

Infrastructure

Days to clear customs to export	Yes	Logs	Average number of days it takes to clear customs when exporting
Days to clear customs to import	Yes	Logs	Average number of days it takes to clear customs when importing
Total duration of power outages	Yes	Logs	Total duration of annual power outages in hours
Losses due to power outages	Yes	%	Losses due to power outages as a percentage of total annual sales
Electricity generator	Yes	Prop.	Proportion of firms using own generator

Red tape, corruption and crime

Manager's time spent with bur. issues	Yes	%	Percentage of total annual manager's time spent dealing with bureaucratic issues
Bribes in taxes	Yes	Prop.	Proportion of firms paying bribes in tax inspections
Bribes to govt. to secure contract	Yes	%	Percentage of contract Value Establishment Pays In Informal payments to secure a contract with the government
Informal payments	Yes	%	Percentage of total annual sales paid in informal payments
Tax inspections	Yes	Log	Annual number of inspections with tax officials
Gifts in tax inspections	Yes	Prop.	Proportion of firms paying bribes in tax inspections
Crime loss or loses due to criminal activity	Yes	%	Percentage of total annual sales lost due to criminal activity
Security	Yes	%	Percentage of total annual sales spent due to security
Informal comp.	Yes	Prop.	Proportion of firms facing informal competition
Auditory	Yes	Prop.	Proportion of firms with external auditory

Finance

Loan	Yes	Prop.	Proportion of firms with a loan
Overdraft	Yes	Prop.	Proportion of firms with an overdraft or line of credit

Table 2 (cont.)

Internal funds financing	Yes	%	Percentage of annual investment financed by internal funds
Equity financing	Yes	%	Percentage of annual investment financed by equity
Sales after delivery	Yes	%	Percentage of total annual sales paid for after delivery

Innovation and labor skills

ISO certified	Yes	Prop.	Proportion of firms with a ISO quality certification
Foreign tech.	Yes	Prop.	Proportion of firms with a foreign licensed technology
Web page use	Yes	Prop.	Proportion of firms using a web page to communicate with clients
New product	Yes	Prop.	Proportion of firms introducing a new product
New process	Yes	Prop.	Proportion of firms introducing a new production process improvement
RND	Yes	Prop.	Proportion of firms with positive R&D investment
RND spend.	Yes	%	Percentage of total annual sales spent in R&D
Training	Yes	Prop.	Proportion of firms providing internal training
Manager's experience	Yes	Logs	Number of years of manager's experience
Skilled workers	Yes	%	Skilled workers as a percentage of total staff
High school workers	Yes	%	Workers with university degree as a percentage of total staff

Other variable control

Age	No	Logs	Firm's age
Pub. listed comp.	No	Dummy	Takes value 1 for publicly listed companies
FDI	No	Dummy	Variable taking value 1 if the firm receives foreign direct investment

(cont.)

Exporter	No	Dummy	Variable taking value 1 if the firm directly exports 10% of total annual sales
Exporting experience	No	Logs	Number of years exporting
Diversification	No	%	Percentage of total annual sales from firm's main product
Owner	No	%	Percentage of firm's value that belongs to the main owner
State owned firm	No	Dummy	Takes value 1 for state owned firms
Importer	No	Dummy	Takes value 1 for firms that import
Local	No	Dummy	Takes value 1 for firms whose main market is local

Four different possible methodological sources were examined as the main causes for obtaining opposite signs of the impact of the IC on TFP in countries such as Guatemala, Honduras and Nicaragua: (1) the decision to pool or not to pool the survey data from different countries, (2) the different levels of aggregation considered within a country (coefficients at the industry or country level), (3) the different TFP estimation procedures considered (GMM, 2SLS, two-stage Solow residuals, structural approaches such as the Olley and Pakes approach, etc.), and (4) the different functional forms of the production functions considered (Translog, Cobb-Douglas, etc.).

The main productivity issues addressed in this Element are the following: Do the signs and order of magnitude of the estimates of IC elasticity in TFP depend primarily on the specific TFP measure used or on the particular TFP estimation procedure considered? What type of econometric methodology can different researchers use to assess the impact of the IC on the TFP, avoiding obtaining contradictory signs of the IC impacts on TFP and the orders of magnitude of the IC coefficients/elasticities on TFP? Is there any aggregate measure of TFP that is valid for international TFP comparisons, avoiding comparing apple and oranges?

In this Element, we will show how to obtain robust signs of IC coefficients on TFP and with a similar order of magnitude of the impacts for several TFP measures. Almost any reasonable TFP measure could be used, as long as the researcher controls for relevant plant-level IC information that affects decisions (avoiding omitted variables). These key variables are usually not observable at the plant level, and are often treated as unobservable fixed effects or random effects by econometricians. This Element shows how ESs provide very rich information at the plant level, allowing for consistent estimates of IC elasticities in TFP that are robust (equal signs and similar order of magnitude) for different TFP measures and for alternative estimation procedures, including ordinary least squares (OLS) on extended production functions.

When any of the inputs to the production function are influenced by common causes that affect TFP, such as IC variables or other unobservable characteristics at the plant level, there is a bias in the estimation of the OLS, or simultaneous equations bias in the estimation of the production functions.[8] This Element assesses the importance of these biases and suggests reducing them by controlling for the set of IC variables in the production function estimation.

The Element is structured as follows. Section 2 introduces the concepts of TFP and discusses the main issues when estimating production function equations and productivity: endogeneity of the inputs, the role of output prices when estimating sales-generating functions and the selection procedure for few IC variables out of a large number of correlated candidates. We also present the econometric methodology for a robust selection of IC and explanatory variables under different productivity measures (TFP). We end this section by discussing the relationship of the structural approach of estimating production functions with our extended production functions estimation. Furthermore, we show in Appendix A that, given the fixed-effect nature of the IC variables obtained from the ESs, it is better to analyze productivity in levels (or logarithmic levels) rather than in productivity growth rates. Section 3 discusses the ES database of Turkey. Important missing data problems are generally found in surveys of emerging and developing countries and we recommended imputation, as opposed to using only the available data (complete case) and available variables with no, or only a few, missing observations. In Section 4, the main empirical results concerning the marginal effects of plant-level IC variables on TFP are included. We present the methodology that allows us to calculate the specific contribution of IC average variables to the average TFP of each country, as well as to determine the allocative efficiency component based on the Olley and

---

[8] There is an extensive body of literature discussing the advantages and disadvantages of using different statistical estimation techniques and/or growth accounting techniques (index number) to estimate productivity or total factor productivity in levels or logs (TFP), or in rates of growth ($\log TFP_t - \log TFP_{t-1} = TFP_t - TFP_{t-1}$). For overviews of different productivity concepts and aggregation alternatives, see Solow (1957), Jorgenson, Gollop and Fraumeni (1987), Hall (1990), Griliches (1996), Olley and Pakes (1996), Foster, Haltiwanger and Krizan (1998), Batelsman and Doms (2000), Hulten (2001), Jorgenson (2001), Diewert and Nakamura (2003), Barro and Sala-i-Martin (2004), Ackerberg et al., (2007), Fried, Lovell and Schmidt (2008), Green (2008) and Grifell-Tatjé and Lovell (2015).

Pakes (1996) productivity decomposition. A new concept of IC-related TFP is introduced, named TFP^{IC}, that allows us to do cross-country comparisons of productivity. We study the strong relationship of TFP^{IC} with other country economic performance measures, such as GDP per capita, doing business scores and global competitiveness index (GCI). Section 5 tests the robustness of the empirical IC results with alternative TFP measures and, in particular, analyzes the case of Turkey using ESs (2018). We end up showing the stability of the TFP^{IC} empirical distribution under eight different TFP measures. Section 6 reviews selected IC assessments of other emerging countries from other regions: Asia, Latin America and the Caribbean (LAC) and Africa. Finally, in Section 8, there is a summary of the main conclusions and possible extensions of this work.

2 Econometric Productivity Methodologies at the Firm Level

The development of a *robust TFP specification strategy* that could be used as a benchmark for the comparison of alternative studies of the impact of IC variables on business productivity in emerging countries is another objective of this Element. By robust TFP methodology we mean one that provides economically similar empirical results on the impact of the IC on TFP; that is, with equal signs of the IC variables and similar orders of magnitude for several alternative TFP measures. This property is essential for making international comparisons.[9]

In particular and as we will see, our estimates for Turkey are robust across eight different measures of TFP from (1) different *functional forms* of production functions, (2) *different estimates of TFPs* and (3) *different levels of aggregation of input-output* elasticities (at the industry and country levels).

We will consider two different approaches to show the *robustness of the empirical results of the IC on TFP*. First, showing that the signs of all IC effects on TFP are usually the same for all the TFP measures used (i.e., there is never a contradiction between coefficients of significant IC variables of different

---

[9] This productivity methodology has been applied in World Bank assessment reports on investment climate impact in more than forty-two developing and emerging countries. This list of countries includes Algeria, Bangladesh, Bolivia and Guatemala, Botswana, Brazil, Burkina Faso, Cameroon, Chile, Colombia, Costa Rica, Croatia, Ecuador, Egypt, El Salvador,Eritrea, Ethiopia, Honduras, Honduras, India, Indonesia, Kenya, Madagascar, Malawi, Mali, Mauritania, Mauritius, Mexico, Morocco, Namibia, Nicaragua, Niger, Pakistan, Pakistan, Peru Philippines, Senegal, South Africa, Swaziland, Tanzania, Turkey, Uganda and Zambia, among others. The robustness properties of the empirical IC results on TFP, presented here for Turkey, are also maintained in all of these countries.

specifications).[10] Second, it is found that the cumulative density and distribution functions of the TFP, after being centered on 0, are similar for most of the TFP measures.

Since there is no single, commonly accepted measure of TFP, any empirical assessment of the impact on productivity (TFP) of IC variables may depend critically on how it is measured. To avoid having to select a particular measure of TFP for policy analysis on productivity, we suggest that robust empirical results of the impact of the IC be sought by using several measures of TFP. This philosophy of robustness of empirical results is endorsed by Ackerberg et al. (2007) when they note: "Finding that the parameters of the production function are consistent across multiple estimation procedures, under different assumptions, is surely more convincing than using just one procedure."

To this end, in this Element we will use eight productivity measures (TFPs) that fit well with the characteristics of our dataset: two levels of aggregation (restricted and unrestricted), with two parametric production functions (Cobb-Douglas and the Translog), with Solow residues for the two levels of aggregation, and applying the structural estimators Levinshon and Petrin (2003) and Ackerberg, Caves and Frazer (2015) (hereinafter, LP and AC&F).

2.1 Alternative Approaches to TFP Estimation

TFP measures the effects of any variable other than inputs – labor (L), intermediate materials (M) and capital services (K) – which affect the production process (or sales).

Let the general production function be $Y_{it} = F(L_{it}, M_{it}, K_{it}; \alpha) TFP_{it}$ where the total factor productivity component is indicated by the variable TFP_{it}. Individual plants/firms are distinguished by the subscript $i = 1, 2, \ldots, N$, where N *is* the total number of plants/firms in the sample and by the subscript time $t = 1, 2, \ldots, T$, where T *is* the total number of years in the sample.[11]

To address the usual endogeneity problem of the inputs (L, M and K) consider the following simple Cobb-Douglas-type of production function model (1),[12]

---

[10] Translog's unrestricted (by industry) production function has too many parameters and is known to give unstable numerical results (due to multicollinearity, nonlinearity, etc.). However, we demonstrated in all international applications made that using the productivity methodology described in this Element, when there are changes, only some coefficients of the IC variables change. When this happens, those IC variables are not significant in those specifications.

[11] In IC and ES surveys, N is large and T is small. The *small letters* indicate that the variables are in logarithms (logs). For example, $logY_{it} = y_{it}$.

[12] See Appendix A for a general discussion of the advantages or disadvantages of alternative analyses, in levels or differences, of multifactor productivity (MFP) or TFP measures. Here we use a broad concept of productivity and call it TFP, with intermediate materials (M) as an input. Some authors in the productivity literature call this concept total productivity (TP) and they leave TFP for the value-added equations. The reason for using it in the formulation of equation (1a) of

$$y_{it} = \alpha_L l_{it} + \alpha_M m_{it} + \alpha_K k_{it} + tfp_{it} \tag{1}$$

$$tfp_{it} = \alpha_p + v_{it} + e_{it}, \tag{2}$$

where $E(tfp_{it}/l_{it}, m_{it}, k_{it}, \alpha) \neq 0 \ldots$ However, $E(e_{it}/l_{it}, m_{it}, k_{it}, v_{it}, \alpha) = 0$ in equation (3) conditioning on an unobservable explanatory variable (v_{it}) that measures unobservable productivity shocks,

$$y_{it} = \alpha_L l_{it} + \alpha_M m_{it} + \alpha_K k_{it} + \alpha_p + v_{it} + e_{it}. \tag{3}$$

That is, the explanatory variables or inputs (L, M and K) are "exogenous" after conditioning them to unobservable productivity shocks.

Our TFP estimation procedure is justified on the basis of the following *simplified model of simultaneous equations (SEM)*. Let (4) be a more explicit Cobb-Douglas production function and (5) the equation incorporating the IC determinants that are usually unobservable in other databases,

$$y_{it} = \alpha_L l_{it} + \alpha_M m_{it} + \alpha_K k_{it} + \alpha_p + v_{it} + e_{it}. \tag{4}$$

$$v_{it} = \alpha_{it} + \zeta_{it} = \alpha'_{IC} IC_{it} + \alpha'_C C_{it} + \alpha'_{Dj} D_j + \alpha'_{D2} D_t + \zeta_{it}. \tag{5}$$

The IC_{it} and C_{it} of equation (5) are vectors of *plant-level* explanatory variables *for investment climate variables* (IC) *and other control variables* (C), while *the D_{jt} and D_t* are vectors of industry dummies (j) and year dummies (t). Note that time dummies (D_t) capture part of the productivity momentum that is usually captured by considering a first-order autocorrelation process (first-order Markov condition in the structural model) of high persistence.[13]

The usual unobservable firm-level effects, $(\alpha'_{IC} IC_{it} + \alpha'_C C_{it})$ are included in the v_{it} component of equation (4) and are replaced here by the set of observable effects given by the variables IC_{it} and C_{it} in equation (5):

$$y_{it} = \alpha_L l_{it} + \alpha_M m_{it} + \alpha_K k_{it} + \alpha'_{IC} IC_{it} + \alpha'_C C_{it} + \alpha'_{Dj} D_j + \alpha'_{D2} D_t + \alpha_P + u_{it}. \tag{6}$$

Therefore, the extended production function (6) represents *conditional expectation* (7) plus a random error term (u_{it}) that is the sum of unpredictable productivity shocks (ζ_{it}) and idiosyncratic shocks (e_{it}),

---

intermediate materials is because in the empirical applications we will use sales as our dependent variable. Therefore, equation (1a) is a sales-generating equation more than a pure production function, as will be discussed later on. Indeed, authors in the recent literature make explicit the difference between TFPQ (related to output only) or technical efficiency and TFPR or technical efficiency plus prices, Hsieh and Klenow (2009) and Haltiwanger (2016).

[13] We could do this, but as most ICs in developing countries are very unbalanced, we prefer not to lose many observations (firms) by allowing the TFP version AR(1).

$$E(y_{it}/l_{it}, m_{it}, k_{it}, v_t, \alpha) = \alpha_L l_{it} + \alpha_M m_{it} + \alpha_K k_{it} + \alpha'_{IC} IC_{it}$$
$$+ \alpha'_C C_{it} + \alpha'_{Dj} D_j + \alpha'_{Dt} D_t + \alpha_P \qquad (7)$$

$u_{it} = \zeta_{it} + e_{it}$, the random error term of the *extended production function* (6), is assumed not to be conditionally correlated with the explanatory variables L, M, K, IC, C and dummy variables D. That is,

$$E[u_{it}/l_{it}, m_{it}, k_{it}, IC_{it}, C_{it}, D_j, D_t] = 0 \qquad (8)$$

$$\text{and } Var[u_{it}|l_{it}, m_{it}, k_{it}, IC_{it}, C_{it}, D_j, D_t] = \sigma^2_{u,it} \qquad (9)$$

Notice that in equation (8) and equation (9) we are conditioning in the usually unobservable effects, (IC_{it}) and (C_{it}), and in certain industry dummies (D_j) and time dummies (D_t) to obtain the orthogonality condition of the inputs (L, M and K) and the error term (u_{it}).[14] Without conditioning in the variables IC and C, there is a correlation between the regression error and the inputs (L, M and K) coming from the *common causes* generated by the normally unobservable enterprise-level effects IC and C.[15]

This argument applies to other functional forms. For example, consider the extended production function of the Translog production function,

$$y_{it} = \alpha_L l_{it} + \alpha_M m_{it} + \alpha_K k_{it} + \alpha_{LL}(l_{it})^2 + \alpha_{MM}(m_{it})^2 + \alpha_{KK}(k_{it})^2 +$$
$$+ \alpha_{LM} l_{it} m_{it} + \alpha_{LK} l_{it} k_{it} + \alpha_{MK} m_{it} k_{it} + \alpha'_{IC} IC_{it} + \alpha'_C C_{it} + \alpha'_{Dj} D_j$$
$$+ \alpha'_{D2} D_t + \alpha_P + u_{it} \qquad (10)$$

which is only a "local approximation" to the unknown function F(K,L,M;α) and therefore may not give very reliable estimates of global parameters.

The popular two-step approach to estimate the partial effects of IC on TFP could be used if the corresponding TFP measure is obtained from the nonparametric Solow's residuals (Solow, 1957). Solow suggested to measure the input-output elasticities at the firm level and for every year, by the revenue-share of each input. In this Element, we also use growth accounting techniques but, following Hall (1990), we measure the cost-share of each input. In the first step,

---

[14] In all regressions with different TFP measures, we always include seven dummy variables (D_r, r = 1, 2, ..., 7) and a constant term (intercept). That is, we control for eight industry effects (food and beverages, textiles, clothing, wood and furniture, paper and publishing, chemicals, rubber and plastics, nonmetallic products and machinery and equipment – metal products) and two years of simulations for the three years of data.

[15] In the empirical application we also consider the standard errors of the parameters that are robust to the clusters (region-industry) and/or to heteroskedasticity and sometimes also to autocorrelation (HAC) when the data allow it. We have also computed the random effects estimators without significant differences in the results.

equation (11), we obtain the TFP estimate (Solow's residual), where $\bar{s}_j$ is the average of the corresponding cost-shares of each input as the average of the last two years.[16] In the second step, equation (12), we estimate the partial effects of the IC variables on TFP:

$$\hat{tfp}_{it} = y_{it} - \bar{s}_L l_{it} - \bar{s}_M m_{it} - \bar{s}_K k_{it}. \tag{11}$$

$$\hat{tfp}_{it} = a'_{IC} IC_{it} + a'_C C_{it} + a'_{Dj} D_j + a'_{D2} D_t + \alpha_P + w_{it}. \tag{12}$$

The advantage of using Solow's residual is that it does not require the factors or inputs (L, M, K) to be exogenous or the input-output elasticities to be constant. The disadvantage is that it requires constant returns to scale (CRS) and at least competitive factor markets.

Other two-step procedures are also applied when, in the first step, productivity is estimated using the L&P and AC&F algorithms.[17] In the case of the AC&F specification, we used the one-step procedure proposed by Wooldridge (2009) due to the efficiency gains obtained in relation to the standard AC&F procedure. Thus, in the empirical section, we ended up with eight different procedures for estimating the effects of IC on TFP.

Fixed Effects Normally Not Observable

The first sequences of IC surveys of companies carried out by the World Bank were done in a specific year t and asked companies for information on the IC_{it} and C_{it} variables for that year t. However, from the inputs (L, M and K), they were asked for information from three previous years, (t, t-1 and t-2). This allowed the assumption that in those three years, the IC of the company had not changed and one could therefore treat that information as fixed effects observable at company level. That is, $IC_{it} = IC_i$ and $C_{it}=C_i$.

In summary, with recall data on production function variables, the equations to be estimated under different estimation procedures and with observables IC fixed effects are equations (13) and (14),

$$y_{it} = \alpha_L l_{it} + \alpha_M m_{it} + \alpha_K k_{it} + a'_{IC} IC_i + a'_C C_i + a'_{Dj} D_j + a'_{D2} D_t + \alpha_P + u_{it}. \tag{13}$$

---

[16] In the *restricted case* we have $\bar{s}_r = (1/2)(s_{rt} + s_{rt-1})$ for r = L, M and K, where s_{rt} is the corresponding share of the costs of input j in year t and the average is $\bar{s}_r$ calculated over the whole sample for input r. In the *unrestricted case*, the averages are similarly calculated but industry by industry (j); see Tables 1 and 2.

[17] In the case of AC&F estimation, we used the one-step modification proposed by Wooldridge (2009), which has proven to be more efficient.

$$\hat{tfp}_{it} - \alpha'_{IC}IC_i + \alpha'_C C_i + \alpha'_{Dj}D_j + \alpha'_{D2}D_t + \alpha_P + w_{it}. \tag{14}$$

Now that we have several years of cross-section surveys that no longer ask for recall data of the inputs, we can analyze different cases:

(i) Estimate a pure cross-section version of equations (10), (13) and (14) for a particular year. Later on, we can repeat the cross-section analysis for another year and compare the evolution. This is the approach used in this Element for the evaluation of the IC of Turkey.

(ii) Estimate equations (10), (13) and (14) with recall data on the variables of the production function (Y, L, M and K), assuming that the IC generates fixed effects for the years of the recall data, usually two or three years, as was done initially in Escribano and Guasch (2004, 2005) and Escribano, Guasch and Pena (2019).

(iii) Estimate two different versions of equations (10), (13) and (14) for cross-section data maintaining the same information on the production function variables (Y, L, M and K), but changing the information on the IC variables from two different years, as fixed observable effects, but considering different values in for each estimate.

Endogeneity of the Input Variables of the Production Function (PF)

There is an identification problem that separates TFP from the production function (PF) when any of the inputs (L, M or K) of the PF are influenced by common unobservable causes that affect productivity (TFP), such as fixed enterprise effects (Marschak and Andrews, 1944; Griliches and Mairesse, 1997; with recent solutions for the panel data proposed in Ackerberg et al., 2015) This problem creates a bias of simultaneous equations if the parameters are estimated by least squares in the estimation equation (1) to obtain the TFP. However, this input endogeneity problem is significantly reduced by using the estimation of the least squares equation (6) following the approach initially proposed by Escribano and Guasch (2004, 2005). That is, in equation (6) we replace the generally unobserved company-specific fixed effects (which are the main cause of input endogeneity) with a long list of company-specific fixed effects observed in IC studies. Controlling for the largest set of forty IC variables and the characteristics of the plants included in C, see Table 2, we can – under regularity conditions – obtain consistent and unbiased least squares estimators of the PF parameters and the corresponding IC elasticities on TFP in a single step. When some the IC variables are endogenous, the most natural approach is to use two-stage least squares (2SLS) using instrumental variables

(IV). The selection of those instruments is in general done from the list of IC variables that are determined outside the firm and that are highly correlated with endogenous IC variables, to avoid the problems of having weak instruments. In the presence of weak instruments, OLS will usually produce more reliable parameter estimates than 2SLS.[18] However, we believe that the endogeneity issues of certain explanatory variables do not produce large biases since the R^2 of the PF regressions are usually very high and close to 90 percent in extended production functions with a long list of IC explanatory variables.

Note that even if we were only interested in assessing the impact of a particular block of IC variables, say infrastructure, we should not limit the scope of the analysis to just this block lest we face an omitted variables problem. Contrary to what was done in other previous studies of the IC – see, for example, Dollar, Hallward-Driemeier and Mengistae (2003, 2004 and 2005), and Dollar, Shi et al. (2004), in our econometric approach, we initially included (and are therefore controlling for) all IC factors from all the blocks listed in Table 2. This is crucial in that IC variables play the role of proxies for commonly unobservable fixed effects. This is the fundamental feature of the Escribano and Guasch (2004, 2005) econometric methodology and provides strong empirical regularities. If, for example, we try to estimate the impact of such an infrastructure, without controlling for the other blocks of IC variables, we can obtain different signs in certain coefficients due to the biases created by the omitted variables; see Escribano and Guasch (2004, 2005). For a very interesting survey of the main IC analysis undertaken at the World Bank see Dethier, Hirn and Straub (2008).

Role of Output Prices When Estimating Production Functions as a Sales-Generating Equation

The role of prices in equation (15) below deserves special attention. Since the dependent variable is now sales, rather than the units of physical production, it also reflects prices and not only quantities produced. In fact, according to the current literature, the term *sales generation function* seems more appropriate than the production function for equation (4), as in the work of Olley and Pakes (1996), when the dependent variable is sales.

If prices are not identical in all companies, what seems to be a plant with high production might just be an establishment that is charging high prices, which

---

[18] See for example Escribano et al. (2008a) for an application of 2SLS to IC variables. However, since the results were in general very similar when doing OLS in the extended PF, in this Element we present the results without using 2SLS. However, with some of the IC variables, we use the industry-region average because it will reduce the effect of missing observations and also reduce the degree of endogeneity.

may be a consequence of market power (non-zero profit margins) or differences in the quality of the final goods, and not indicating more output. While with homogeneous products, high productivity could be a reflection of high prices or, in other words, a reflection of market power (Bernard et al., 2003; Melitz, 2003; Katayama, Lu and Tybout, 2009; Foster, Haltiwanger and Syverson, 2008), in the case of heterogeneous or differentiated products, high prices could be a consequence of higher quality, which could translate into over-measured productivity, since some plants could produce higher quality and higher priced products with the same amount of production (Levinsohn and Melitz, 2001; Katayama, Lu and Tybout, 2009; de Loecker, 2013). These points are particularly important in developing countries, where market power is generally a serious constraint on aggregate growth. Addressing these issues is not an easy task with the available ESs. A more comprehensive analysis would require information on product prices at plant level to incorporate the demand side of the model.

Until these data are available, a plausible solution is to estimate the system in equations (4)–(5) following a control function approach. Now instead of looking at production (Y), we are looking at sales (P*Y), where P indicates the prices of the products, and therefore equation (4) becomes equation (15),

$$\log Y_{it} + \log P_{it} = \log P_{it} + \alpha_L \log L_{it} + \alpha_M \log M_{it} + \alpha_K \log K_{it} + \log TFP_{it}.$$
(15)

It is important to note that while we control for $logP_{it}$ on the right side of equation (15), the marginal effect on the *log of* revenues ($\log Y_{it} + \log P_{it}$), remains the same as the effect on $logTFP_{it}$. Otherwise, instead of estimating technical efficiency or TFP, we would be estimating a compound term, logTFPR= logTFP+logP or TFPR= TFP*P, in which case the estimated positive (negative) marginal effects on TFPR could come from improvements (worsening) in technical efficiency or from positive (negative) effects on prices due to the market power of the firms and/or the quality of the products. Indeed, examples in the recent literature make explicit the difference between TFPQ or technical efficiency and TFPR or technical efficiency plus prices: see Hsieh and Klenow (2009) and Haltiwanger (2016).

Since within one year there is low price variability at the company level not related to the IC, we can assume that $logP_{it}$ can be replaced by a term at the company level $logIC_{it}$, the control variables C_i which are fixed-effect vectors, at the company level and a set of dummy variables, Dit, which include the region, industry and year dummy vectors. Therefore, after controlling for all these observable effects, if we assume that $\log P_{it} \approx g(IC_{it}, D_j, D_t)$ on the right-hand side of equation (15), we can obtain an expression similar to equation (15) that incorporates the revenues from sales ($Y_{it}P_{it}$) instead of the production (Y_{it}). That is,

$$\log(Y_{it}P_{it}) = \alpha_L \log L_{it} + \alpha_M \log M_{it} + \alpha_K \log K_{it} + \alpha'_{IC}IC_{it} + \alpha'_C IC_{it}$$
$$+ \alpha'_{Dj}D_j + \alpha'_{D2}D_t + \alpha_P + \log TFP_{it} \tag{16}$$

Under these assumptions, estimating sales with equation (16), as we do in our empirical analysis of the IC, can provide estimates of TFP that can be "interpreted" as effects on "technical efficiency".[19] Finally, to control for profit margin (market power effect) and/or quality (differentiated products), we also include several IC and C variables related to competition (see Table 2 for the list of IC variables included in the group of other control variables).[20]

Strategies for the Selection of IC Variables

The econometric methodology applied for the selection of the variables IC and C goes from the general to the specific. For an automatic modelling of this specification process see Hendry and Krolzig (2001, 2003) and Escribano and Sucarrat (2012). Once we have a parsimonious model with only significant IC variables from different IC blocks, we will check that there are no omitted IC variables, following Escribano and Guasch (2004, 2005), for example, to make sure that we have not eliminated the relevant IC variables due to the strong multicollinearity of the initial general model.

The problem of the *omitted variables* we found, from estimating a too-simple model, generates biased and inconsistent parameter estimates. Conversely, adding *irrelevant variables* (that is, from a very general model with some variables that are irrelevant) could suffer from multicollinearity among IC variables that provide unbiased and consistent, but inefficient, estimates. Therefore, we start from a general model, such as equation (6), with most of the forty IC variables included at once, and reduce this general model to a simpler model with only relevant (meaningful) variables.[21] We also then

---

[19] Note, however, that the term *technical efficiency* is too specific, as there are many efficiencies related to the TFP^{IC} variables that are not technical (regulatory, governance, institutional, etc.).

[20] A good way to check whether productivity measures can be driven by market power and prices is to compare the productivities of different market structures – monopolies, duopolies, oligopolies or fragmented market types; local, national, international – sizes, sectors and states. We believe that, in addition to the monitoring approach followed, this type of analysis can help us identify whether measured productivities may be driven by margins and/or differentiated products rather than by differences in efficiency. See Escribano et al. (2009) for an example of this type of analysis.

[21] Sometimes, in the final regression model, we leave the IC variables that are not individually significant but are relevant to the model, either because they have a significant effect in

start adding IC variables to the selected model (from the particular to the general) to check if we have omitted any relevant IC variables in the process (specification checks). The estimation of the final model is more efficient once we have eliminated the irrelevant variables.

As we have discussed, with linear models it is usually recommended to go from the general to the specific to avoid omitted variable biases and to discard estimating spurious correlations. Hendry and Nielsen (2007) consider a regression with *n irrelevant variables* and conclude that the average of variables that are significant by chance at the significant level of α, is $n\alpha$. Let us say that $\alpha = 0.05$ and $n = 40$ *and* then $n\alpha = 2$. That is, on average, two irrelevant variables are included and thirty-eight relevant variables are correctly excluded if *the contrast of the repeated t-ratio is used*. If α is reduced to $\alpha = 0.01$, as sometimes suggested when doing the repeated t-test, and $n = 40$ then the average number of significant variables is reduced to $n\alpha = 0.4$. However, the main problem with reducing the level of significance α, is that we are also reducing the power of t-ratio based contrast, which makes it difficult to detect the relevant variables (which is a miss-specification with crucial implications in terms of spurious correlations). The Monte Carlo evidence from Hoover and Perez (1999) and Hendry and Krolzig (2001, 2005), shows that modeling from the general to the specific has a small search cost; that is, a small additional cost in terms of size and power that arises when performing repeated tests with multipath selection algorithms from a general unrestricted model (GUM). Notice that GUM is not the true local data generating process (DGP), Escribano and Sucarrat (2012).

In the process of reduction, we do not eliminate all the nonsignificant variables at once, since, due to multicollinearity, if we eliminate a variable that is highly correlated with others, some of the nonsignificant variables may become highly correlated. An informative statistic for this purpose is the R^2 variation of the regression (or even better, the residual standard error). We apply the iterative procedure, eliminating the less-significant variables leaving, for interpretative purposes, at least one IC variable from each block of ICs in Table 2 (infrastructure, bureaucracy/corruption, crime, finance, innovation and human capital, other control variables). Once we have a reasonably parsimonious model, we start to test if there are IC variables omitted block by block, to see if, due to the existence of multicollinearity between IC variables, we have eliminated a relevant IC variable. Notice that most automatic modeling processes do not follow all these back and forth steps, block by block, going also from the specific to the general. The reason is that they are based on orthogonal regressors and therefore multicollinearity problems do not arise in this context.

---

conjunction with other variables or they are significant in other TFP measures. When this occurs, it may be due to the presence of multicollinearity between some of the explanatory variables of the production function (especially in the case of Translog) or between other IC variables.

2.2 A Comparison of the IC Extended Production Function Approach with Structural Production Function Approaches

Structural methods for estimating production functions have gained popularity in recent years, starting with Olley and Pakes (1996) (hereinafter, O&P), with key contributions from L&P and AC&F, Wooldridge (2009) and de Loecker (2013). In all cases, the estimation is based on the use of delayed input choices as instruments, and they share some similarities and divergences with the model proposed here. Since AC&F covers the main characteristics of O&P and L&P, we focus on this method for comparison with the model proposed here.

The structural model in AC&F can be written in this case as

$$y_{it} = \alpha_L l_{it} + \alpha_K k_{it} + v_{it} + e_{it} \tag{17}$$

$$v_{it} = \Psi[v_{it-1}] + \alpha_P + \xi_{it} \tag{18}$$

$$v_{it} = f_t^{-1}(m_{it}, k_{it}, l_{it}). \tag{19}$$

The unobserved productivity (v_{it}) for both production functions, equations (18) and (19), is replaced by two different approaches based on two different sets of information. While AC&F requires certain types of dynamic panel structure, our approach can be used on simple cross sections or on dynamic panels with trend data but uncorrelated errors.[22] The corresponding extended production functions are:

$$y_{it} = \alpha_L l_{it} + \alpha_K k_{it} + \Psi\left[f_{t-1}^{-1}(m_{it-1}, k_{it-1}, l_{it-1})\right] + \alpha_P + \xi_{it} + e_{it}. \tag{20}$$

However, following AC&F, equation (20) requires a two-step approach; first, an estimate of f(.) and Ψ using equations (18) and (19), and second, a final estimate of α_L, the α_K using sample analogs following two orthogonality conditions. Note that none of the structural TFP, O&P, L&P or AC&F estimation procedures allow for consideration of fixed effects in equation (20).

---

[22] The corresponding equation (17), in the traditional dynamic panel literature of Chamberlain (1982), Arellano and Bond (1991) and Blundell and Bond (1998, 2000), is the following: where an AR(1) process is followed, where $v_{it} = a_i + \alpha'_{Ds}D_j + \omega_{it} + \alpha_P + \xi_{it}$ and $\omega_{it} = \rho\omega_{it-1} + \zeta_{it}$, where the AR(1) ($\rho$) coefficient is high and close to one (persistent productivity shocks). In our approach, this high AR(1) is replaced by a flexible deterministic trend with changing coefficients given by the time dummy variables $\alpha'_{D2}D_t$.

From now on, our *base model* for carrying out robustness tests will be the extended production function (6).[23] For this purpose, equations (6) and (20) can be nested in the model (21):

$$y_{it} = \alpha_L l_{it} + \alpha_K k_{it} + \Psi\left[f_{t-1}^{-1}(m_{it-1}, k_{it-1}, l_{it-1})\right] + \alpha'_{IC}IC_{Pi}$$
$$+ \alpha'_C C_{Pi} + \alpha'_{Ds}D_{1j} + \alpha'_{D2}D_{2t} + \alpha_P + e_{it} \tag{21}$$

This nested model allows us to test whether our IC elasticity estimates of equation (6) differ by adding the cubic polynomial approximations suggested by the L&P procedure. The results will be discussed later in the empirical section.[24]

Another option, initially suggested in de Loecker (2013), is to extend the Markovian process of productivity in equation (12). The idea of de Loecker (2013) is to allow the Markov process to include other factors related with productivity, that is, to make the motion equation endogenous. In the original paper, de Loecker (2013) extends the equation by including learning by exporting; in terms of the IC variables analyzed in this Element, the motion equation could be written as

$$v_{it} = \Psi[v_{it-1}, IC_{ir-1}, C_{ir-1}] + \alpha_P + \xi_{it}, \tag{22}$$

where the method allows for some flexibility in the functional form of ψ[.]. In a recent application, Cusolito, Lederman and Pena (2020) use a fully third-degree polynomial to estimate the effects of digital adoption of productivity. The coefficients of the production function can be estimated along with e_{it} in a first step, to generate a measure of productivity as

$$\hat{v}_{it} = y_{it} - \hat{\alpha}_L l_{it} - \hat{\alpha}_K k_{it} - \hat{e}_{it}, \tag{23}$$

which can be used to recover the effects of the IC variables in productivity through

---

[23] Heterogeneous and time-varying input-output elasticities ($\alpha_{j,it}$) could be estimated by nonparametric procedures, index number techniques (Solow 1957, Diewert and Nakamura 2003) or estimated by regression techniques assuming constant input and output elasticity parameters. In this Element, we will examine two options: (1) the *unconstrained* case in which the constant input and output elasticities are assumed to vary at the *industry level*, and (2) the *restricted* case in which the parameters of elasticity are assumed to be constant at the *aggregate level*: see Table 9.

[24] Note the differences between OP, LP and ACF. OP uses an investment equation to identify $f^{-1}(.)$, but both OP and LP estimate the elasticity of labor in a first stage assuming fully flexible labor. The innovation of ACF is to identify all the coefficients in a second stage assuming labor is quasi-fixed.

$$\hat{v}_{it} = \hat{\Psi}[v_{it-1}, IC_{ir-1}, C_{ir-1}] + \alpha_p + \xi_{it}. \tag{24}$$

Table 6d shows the results of the de Loecker (2013) approach using ES data and assuming a linear form for equation (24). Note that the number of observations used changes since the method loses one cross section as it uses lagged variables in equation (24).

3 Enterprise Surveys and Imputation of Missing Observations

A common feature of many enterprise-level databases for developing countries is the presence of a large percentage of missing values on variables measuring enterprise performance. In the case of the sample used for Turkey 2018, there is complete information for sales and only 0.3 percent of the employment data is missing. However, the amount of missing data increases to 37.3 percent for intermediate consumption and 29.2 percent for the capital stock. The problem is common to many IC variables. While the information available for many of the required variables is complete, for many other variables the response rate drops to 70 percent; see Table 3. Selecting the best model specification with only the available observations, the complete case of Turkey 2018 would imply using only 290 of the 1,112 observations, only 26 percent of the original sample size of the survey. The trade-off, if we do not want to miss that many observations, is to drop some variables with a high percentage of missing values from the list of forty given in Table 3, facing therefore an important omitted-variables problem that could generate biases in all the parameter estimates.

The most common solution to the problem of missing values is to eliminate those variables with response rates that are too low. However, in models such as the one presented in this Element, where the idea of controlling for the relevant firm level information is so important, omitting relevant variables could result in biases in estimating the effects of other variables that are included in the TFP model.

The standard econometric approach is to work with the complete case. As we have mentioned before, in the case of Turkey this would imply starting the process of variable selection with only 26 percent of the original sample size. This model selection process is likely to generate important biases if the sample selection is endogenous. Our imputation process overcomes this problem as will be explained: see also Pena (2009) and Pena and Escribano (2021).

For production function variables in developing countries, the process of sample selection, or available variable observations is most likely endogenous. The firms that report all production function information (Y, L, M and K) and all

Table 3 Lost observations and main moments of the variables of the production function and IC of the Turkey 2018 ES

Variable name	Non-missing	Perc.	Mean	St. Dev.
Revenue (ln)	1,112	100.0	16.07	1.50
Employment (ln)	1109	99.7	11.15	1.39
Materials (ln)	697	62.7	14.09	1.81
Capital stock (ln)	787	70.8	14.39	2.09
Labor cost (ln)	830	74.6	13.56	1.33
Days to clear customs to export	292	26.3	1.15	0.63
Days to clear customs to import	118	10.6	1.31	0.67
Total duration of power outages (ln)	1054	94.8	0.33	0.78
Losses due to power outages (%)	1076	96.8	0.70	3.20
Electricity generator	1,111	99.9	0.30	0.46
Manager's time spent with bur. issues	1067	96.0	7.50	14.11
Bribes in taxes	1100	98.9	0.00	0.05
Bribes to govt. To secure contract	1098	98.7	0.06	1.24
Infomal payments	1,112	100.0	3.89	19.16
Tax inspections	1088	97.8	0.82	3.42
Crime loss	1108	99.6	0.01	0.20
Security	1109	99.7	0.49	0.50
Informal comp.	1090	98.0	0.38	0.48
Auditory	1094	98.4	0.34	0.47
Loan	1,112	100.0	0.38	0.49
Overdraft	1,112	100.0	0.79	0.41
Internal funds financing	1043	93.8	18.23	36.78
Equity financing	1042	93.7	0.72	6.71
Sales after delivery	785	70.6	39.76	29.02
ISO certified	1,112	100.0	0.48	0.50
Foreign tech.	1,112	100.0	0.13	0.34
Web page use	1,112	100.0	0.74	0.44
New product	1104	99.3	0.09	0.29
New process	1099	98.8	0.03	0.16
RND	1,112	100.0	0.08	0.27
RND spend.	1094	98.4	0.16	2.02
Training	1,112	100.0	0.36	0.48
Manager's experience	1103	99.2	3.16	0.56
Skilled workers	873	78.5	44.66	22.63
High school workers	961	86.4	47.11	35.36
Age	1,112	100.0	2.85	0.69

Table 3 (cont.)

Variable name	Non-missing	Perc.	Mean	St. Dev.
Pub. listed comp.	1,112	100.0	0.71	0.45
IDF	1,112	100.0	0.03	0.17
Exporter	1,112	100.0	0.27	0.44
Exporting experience	1,112	100.0	4.94	9.77
Diversification	1,112	100.0	95.77	11.39
Owner	1,112	100.0	75.43	26.12
State owned firm	1,112	100.0	0.01	0.07
Importer	1,112	100.0	0.12	0.32
Local	1,112	100.0	0.41	0.49

Source: Authors' estimates with data from the Turkey 2018 ES).

IC information are usually large firms, the most productive firms that are capable of carrying out detailed and systematized accounting of internal decisions. These firms are usually the most efficient. If this is true, the selection will depend on the companies' TFP. Since the full case eliminates any cross-section variable with at least one missing value, it is very likely that the full case will only include companies with high TFP on average. This problem of endogenous sample selection generates a serious problem of bias and inconsistent parameter estimates.

There are five main reasons to use imputation of missing values in a regression context like the one of this Element: increase the sample size, avoid endogenous sample selection problems, eliminate biases due to omitted relevant variables, prevent missing observations form affecting the selection of relevant IC variables, and also produce efficiency gains in the estimation.

In this Element, we suggest using the *fully conditional specification* (FCS) method of van Buuren et al. (2006) and Raghunathan et al. (2001) to impute missing observations in both production function variables and IC variables. Pena and Escribano (2020) offer Monte Carlo simulation evidence on the advantages of this structural imputation process using the FCS algorithm. They show that there is an important reduction in biases of parameter estimates relative to working with the complete case. This is especially relevant when the sample selection is endogenous and affects the dependent variable as well as the explanatory variables.

Table 4 illustrates that FCS imputation is important for the estimation of the input-output elasticities of the production function variables. The complete case, taking into account the missing observations of the IC variables, involves using

Table 4 Production function parameter estimates with and without imputation

		Complete case	Imputed sample
Employment			
(L)	**Coefficient**	0.184***	0.23***
	Standard error	(0.051)	(0.032)
Materials			
(M)	**Coefficient**	0.599***	0.444***
	Standard error	(0.039)	(0.053)
Capital			
(K)	**Coefficient**	0.007	0.10***
	Standard error	(0.03)	(0.02)
R^2		0.83	0.73
Sample size (N)		290	1,112

Source: Authors' estimates with data from the Turkey 2018 ES.

only 290 observations. In the imputed sample, we can use the complete sample of 1,112 observations. In the example shown in Table 4, the capital stock coefficient is not statistically significant, while in the imputed sample the coefficient is significant at 1 percent and it is equal to 0.10, which is a more-reliable value given the existing production function parameter estimates in the literature.

The FCS method proposes to extract candidate values to replace the missing observations from the set of conditional density functions of the variables. The idea of the FCS approach is to use a Gibbs Sampler to iterate R times through the set of conditional variables to fill (impute) the missing observations. The algorithm imputes all the variables each time the IC parameters are estimated in the extended production function regression, starting with the complete list of forty IC variables of Table 2. In each iteration step, the IC variable with the lowest t-ratio is removed from the model and the new model is imputed again. In the final step, our FCS process imputes the missing values of the production function variables (Y, L, M and K) and the missing values of the significant IC variables.

Table 5 gives details of the means and standard deviations of the variables used in the final imputation. The imputation method works well, since there are no statistically significant differences between the sample groups. If we focus on the two variables from the production function with the highest percentage of missing values, materials (M) and capital stock (K), the imputed sample preserves both the mean and the standard deviation of both variables.

Section 4.1 shows more empirical results based on comparing the IC impacts on TFP; in particular, when estimation is done for Turkey using the imputed sample (Table A.1), and using the complete case (Table A.2). Evidence is in favor of using

Table 5 Mean and standard deviation of the variables before and after imputation

Variable	Before imputation				After imputation	
	Non-missing	Perc.	Mean	St. Dev.	Mean	St. Dev.
Revenue (log)	1,112	100.0	16.07	1.50	16.07	1.50
Employment (log)	1,109	99.7	11.15	1.39	11.16	1.39
Materials (log)	697	62.7	14.09	1.81	14.38	1.85
Capital stock (log)	787	70.8	14.39	2.09	14.38	2.15
Electricity generator	1,111	99.9	0.30	0.46	0.30	0.46
Crime loss.	1,108	99.6	0.01	0.20	0.01	0.20
Security	1,109	99.7	0.49	0.50	0.49	0.50
Tax inspections	1,088	97.8	0.82	3.42	0.83	3.40
Informal comp.	1,090	98.0	0.38	0.48	0.38	0.48
Bribes in taxes	1,100	98.9	0.00	0.05	0.00	0.05
Equity financing	1,042	93.7	0.72	6.71	0.92	6.65
Sales after delivery	785	70.6	39.76	29.02	39.19	28.54
Web page use	1,112	100.0	0.74	0.44	0.74	0.44
Training	1,112	100.0	0.36	0.48	0.36	0.48
Age	1,112	100.0	2.85	0.69	2.85	0.69

Source: Authors' estimates with data from Turkey 2018 ES.

imputation for ESs from emerging countries, and specially for the less-developed countries where the quality of the data is very low and there is a high percentage of missing values in both the IC and production function variables.

4 Empirical Results on the Impact of IC Variables on TFP in Turkey

As noted in the previous sections of this Element, the main purpose of this work is to obtain *sound empirical international IC effects on productivity.* For that, the robustness property of the empirical IC effects on alternative TFP measures is key. Here we apply the previous TFP methodologies to the case of firm-level data from the Turkey 2018 ES. The natural question that arises at this point is: what can we learn from the econometric analysis of TFP about the main constraints related to the IC facing firms in Turkey? To answer this question, we start by presenting the results obtained using the Turkey 2018 ES and compare them with the results obtained ten years before with the Turkey 2008 ES of Escribano et al. (2008a and 2008b).

4.1 Marginal IC Effects on TFP Based on Turkey 2019 ES and Turkey 2007 ES

First, starting from the elasticities and semi-elasticities of the IC over the TFP shown in Table 2,[25] we have selected thirteen significant IC and C variables for Turkey 2018 ES, listed in Figure 2a which shows the coefficients of each variable. These marginal effects of IC on TFP shown are obtained using the general-to-specific model selection strategy described in previous sections. In Figure 2b, we only include the set of IC variables that were *significant in at least one of the eight TFP specifications*. Detailed empirical results will be discussed in the next sections.

The full robust estimates to eight productivity measures are included in Table 6a after imputation of missing values. Notice that the IC results on the eight measures of TFP are robust (when the IC variables are significant they always have similar numerical values and the same sign). The effects of the IC are organized into five groups; one variable in the Infrastructure group (electricity generator), five variables within the Bureaucracy, Corruption and Crime group (crime loss, security, tax inspections, informal competition and bribes in taxes), two variables in the Finance group (equity financing and sales after delivery), two variables in the Innovation and Labor skills group (Web page use, training), and one variable in the Other Control Variables group (age of the firms). The interpretation of the effects is done, as usual, in *ceteris paribus* terms, so what matters is the statement "for companies facing the same investment climate conditions, the same input levels and operating in the same industry and the same year the effect of an increase in one of the 13 IC variables is . . .."

In addition, it is important to note that the interpretation of the partial effects when the IC variables are measured as an industry-region average is slightly different from the usual case when the IC variables are measure at the firm/plant level. A change in industry-region averages can be interpreted as an improvement in the overall IC conditions of the region and industry that affect businesses, see Escribano, Guasch and Pena (2019) for detailed individual economic interpretations of the impact of each IC variable on TFP of several countries.

---

[25] The economic interpretation of each climate investment coefficient depends on the units of measurement of each IC variable and the transformations carried out on them (logarithms, fractions, percentages, qualitative constructions, etc.). Since all productivity measures (TFP) considered here are always in logs, when the variable IC is also expressed in logs, the estimated coefficient measures the constant *elasticity of the IC over the TFP*. When the variable IC is not expressed in logs and is not a binary variable, the estimated coefficient is usually described as the *semi-elasticity of the IC in the TFP*. While it is sometimes natural to express an IC variable in logs, for some types of IC variables it is more appropriate not to do so; for example, when an IC variable is a fraction or percentage number with some data equal to or close to 0. Note, however, that expressing IC variables as fractions allows us to also interpret their coefficients as constant elasticities rather than semi-elasticities.

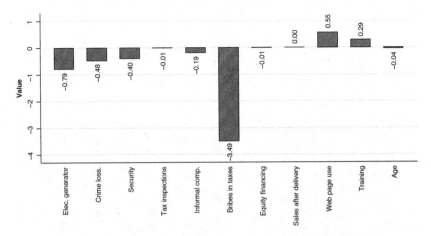

Figure 2a Robust coefficients of IC variables on TFP in Turkey 2018 ES

Note: The coefficients are those of the two-step specification using the restricted Solow residual as the dependent variable.

Source: Authors' estimates with data from Turkey 2018 ES.

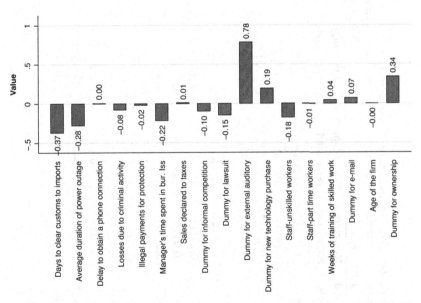

Figure 2b Robust IC effects on TFP, restricted estimation, based on Turkey 2008 ES

Source: Escribano et al. (2008a) estimates with data fromTurkey 2008 ES.

Similarly, Table 6b shows the IC results on the eight different TFP estimates using the *complete case*, that is, using only the available observations without imputation of missing values in any variable. The main conclusion is that the

Table 6a Robust IC estimations on TFP *with imputation* of missing values based on Turkey 2018 ES

| | Two Steps | | Single Step | | | | Two Steps | |
Variable	Restricted Solow res.	Restricted Solow res.	Cobb-Douglas restricted	Cobb-Douglas Unrestricted	Translog restricted	Translog unrestricted	LP	ACF
Electricity generator	-0.789***	-0.766***	-0.440*	-0.420*	-0.597**	-0.531**	-0.573**	-0.748***
	(0.196)	(0.196)	(0.194)	(0.187)	(0.183)	(0.185)	(0.192)	(0.192)
Losses due to criminal activity	-0.479***	-0.423***	-0.378***	-0.363**	-0.483***	0.00288	-0.468***	-0.401***
	(0.0630)	(0.0647)	(0.0845)	(0.112)	(0.115)	(0.325)	(0.0591)	(0.0624)
Security	-0.399	-0.402**	-0.204	-0.0927	-0.201	-0.0679	-0.222	-0.408**
	(0.209)	(0.203)	(0.242)	(0.263)	(0.230)	(0.270)	(0.218)	(0.211)
Tax inspections	-0.0121	-0.0115	-0.00970	-0.0121	-0.0105**	-0.00829	-0.00946	-0.0119**
	(0.0110)	(0.0104)	(0.00775)	(0.00713)	(0.00784)	(0.00623)	(0.00943)	(0.00994)
Informal comp.	-0.187	-0.175	-0.317	-0.452*	-0.436*	-0.674**	-0.322	-0.223
	(0.183)	(0.180)	(0.167)	(0.208)	(0.168)	(0.223)	(0.174)	(0.181)
Bribes in taxes	-3.492**	-3.286**	-2.576*	-2.416	-2.057	-0.993	-2.740*	-3.688***
	(1.057)	(1.054)	(1.230)	(1.304)	(1.147)	(1.361)	(1.066)	(1.029)
Equity financing	-0.00931***	-0.00945***	0.00642**	0.00545*	-0.00693***	0.00676**	-0.00715***	-0.00917***
	(0.00176)	(0.00172)	(0.00203)	(0.00250)	(0.00186)	(0.00207)	(0.00187)	(0.00174)

	(1)	(2)	(3)	(4)	(5)	(6)	(7)	(8)
Sales after delivery	0.000450	0.000454	0.000982	0.000309	0.000571	0.0000866	0.000970	0.000304
	(0.00101)	(0.00101)	(0.00115)	(0.000989)	(0.00103)	(0.000975)	(0.00104)	(0.000998)
Web page use	0.547*	0.505*	0.446*	0.509*	0.391	0.347	0.472*	0.536*
	(0.228)	(0.224)	(0.208)	(0.213)	(0.208)	(0.238)	(0.211)	(0.225)
Training	0.287	0.295	0.336	0.546**	0.374*	0.375	0.365	0.329
	(0.268)	(0.273)	(0.245)	(0.282)	(0.231)	(0.265)	(0.249)	(0.255)
Age	−0.0375	−0.0347	0.0689	0.0688	0.0422	0.0544	0.0427	−0.0227
	(0.0397)	(0.0398)	(0.0442)	(0.0389)	(0.0426)	(0.0405)	(0.0383)	(0.0397)
N	1,112	1,112	1,112	1,112	1,112	1,112	1,112	1,112
R^2	0.140	0.134	0.727	0.746	0.767	0.790	0.157	0.134

Notes: *significant at 10%; ** significant at 5%; *** significant at 1%. Each regression includes a set of industry dummies, year dummmies and a constant term.

Source: Authors' estimates with data from Turkey 2018 ES.

Table 6b Robust IC estimations on TFP without imputation of missing values based on Turkey 2018 ES: complete case

	Two Steps		Single step				Two steps	
	Restricted Solow res.	Unrestricted Solow res.	Cobb-Douglas restricted	Cobb-Douglas Unrestricted	Translog restricted	Translog unrestricted	LP	ACF
Electricity generator	−0.837*	−0.765*	−0.550	−0.373	−0.538*	−0.630*	−0.570	−0.795*
	(−2.37)	(−2.12)	(−1.94)	(−1.22)	(−2.19)	(−2.15)	(−1.83)	(−2.40)
Losses due to criminal activity	−0.0581	−0.0431	0.369	0.413	0.307*	0.524	0.154	0.0590
	(−0.16)	(−0.12)	(1.57)	(1.09)	(2.02)	(1.65)	(0.53)	(0.18)
Security	−0.0262	−0.0400	0.118	0.0286	0.114	0.177	0.354	−0.00550
	(−0.06)	(−0.09)	(0.31)	(0.06)	(0.35)	(0.43)	(0.90)	(−0.01)
Tax inspections	−0.0101	−0.0123	0.0166	−0.00441	0.0286	0.0255	0.0287	−0.00550
	(−0.20)	(−0.26)	(0.33)	(−0.07)	(0.84)	(0.60)	(0.56)	(−0.11)
Informal comp.	−0.304	−0.296	−0.548	−0.529	−0.432	−0.766	−0.425	−0.375
	(−0.89)	(−0.85)	(−1.72)	(−1.55)	(−1.40)	(−1.99)	(−1.36)	(−1.14)
Bribes in taxes	−0.0403	0.0942	0.372	−0.552	0.829	0.109	0.720	−0.0550
	(−0.02)	(0.05)	(0.22)	(−0.29)	(0.54)	(0.05)	(0.39)	(−3.03)
Equity financing	−0.00534**	−0.00529**	−0.00359	−0.00224	−0.00417	−0.00294	−0.00375	−0.00515*
	(−2.80)	(−2.78)	(−1.29)	(−0.65)	(−1.41)	(−0.79)	(−1.37)	(−2.56)

Sales after delivery	0.000396	0.000466	0.00117	0.000752	−0.000279	−0.000790	0.00112	0.000548
	(0.28)	(0.33)	(0.89)	(0.56)	(−0.22)	(−0.58)	(0.82)	(0.40)
Web page use	0.524	0.411	0.562*	0.449	0.597*	0.501	0.393	0.545
	(1.78)	(1.33)	(2.11)	(1.34)	(2.62)	(1.63)	(1.49)	(1.97)
Training	−0.257	−0.244	−0.510	−0.251	−0.510	−0.522	−0.513	−0.313
	(−0.53)	(−0.49)	(−1.33)	(−0.58)	(−1.31)	(−1.16)	(−1.20)	(−0.69)
Age	0.00629	0.00540	0.0659	0.0782	0.0923	0.104	0.0782	0.0158
	(0.10)	(0.09)	(1.07)	(1.29)	(1.83)	(1.66)	(1.34)	(0.25)
N	415	415	415	415	415	415	415	415
R^2	0.203	0.196	0.771	0.786	0.827	0.858	0.238	0.198

Notes: *significant at 10%; ** significant at 5%; *** significant at 1%. Each regression includes a set of industry dummies, year dummies and a constant term.

Source: Authors' estimates with data from Turkey 2018 ES.

key usual robustness property of the TFP estimates is lost and many of the IC effects on TFP even change sign depending on TFP measure; see, for example, the coefficients of *crime loss* or *bribes in taxes*, etc. The main message to get from this case is that the quality of the responses of ESs in emerging countries is not very high, having many missing values in key variables (such as the stock of capital, etc.). Therefore, it is very important to impute the missing values to get reliable (unbiased estimates) and robust empirical results to different TFP measures.

The purpose now is to compare the evolution of basic IC results with the information we have from Turkey 2008 ES. The marginal IC effects on TFP obtained from Turkey 2008 ES by Escribano et al. (2008a, 2008b) are included in Table 6c.

The results of the input-output elasticities estimates for five of the main TFP estimates, restricted and unrestricted, are shown in Tables 7 and 8, respectively.

4.2 Effects of Average IC on Average TFP and International Productivity Comparisons Based on TFP^{IC}

While the partial marginal effects of the IC provide an important assessment of a given country's IC conditions, we should go one step further and assess how average IC conditions affect average TFP. This exercise allows us to assess whether or not a given IC factor is important by considering how many firms suffer a bottleneck (e.g., the number of power outages that firms suffer on average). Thus, a given IC factor with a low marginal partial effect may become important if most firms suffer from that particular problem. For example, this is the case of the *Website usage* variable *that* although it has a coefficient on TFP of 0.55. However, since this variable affects many of Turkey's companies, the impact on average TFP is much greater, representing 14.8 percent of the average TFP (see Figure 3).

The idea is as follows; consider the Cobb-Douglas estimated extended equation (6)

$$y_{it} = \hat{a}_1 l_{it} + \hat{a}_2 m_{it} + \hat{a}_3 k_{it} + \hat{a}_1^{IC} IC_{1,i} + \ldots + \hat{a}_r^{IC} IC_{r,i}^* + \hat{a}_C' C_i + \hat{a}_{Ds}' D_j$$
$$+ \hat{a}_{D2}' D_t + \hat{a}_P + \hat{e}_{it} \tag{25}$$

and let TFP be centered on 0 (excluding the constant term) and given by $\hat{tfp}_{it}^d = y_{it} - \hat{a}_L l_{it} - \hat{a}_M m_{it} - \hat{a}_K k_{it} - \hat{a}_P$. Therefore, the estimated TFP centered around 0 is equal to

$$\hat{tfp}_{it}^d = \hat{a}_1^{IC} IC_{1,i} + \ldots + \hat{a}_r^{IC} IC_{r,i} + \hat{a}_C' C_i + \hat{a}_{Ds}' D_j + \hat{a}_{D2}' D_t + \hat{e}_{it}. \tag{26}$$

Evaluating equation (26) on the mean the OLS residual has sample mean equal to 0 and it disappears from the equation, so we obtain equation (27),

Table 6c Robust IC effects on TFP, restricted estimation, based on Turkey 2008 ES

Blocks of IC variables	Explanatory ICA variables	Two-step estimation Solow residual		Single-step estimation Cobb-Douglas		Translog	
		OLS	RE	OLS	RE	OLS	RE
Infrastructures	Days to clear customs to imports (a)	−0.171***	−0.171**	−0.199****	−0.198***	−0.198****	−0.202***
	Average duration of power outages (a)	−0.332***	−0.332***	−0.323***	−0.318****	−0.286****	−0.293***
	Delay to obtain a phone connection (a)	−0.005**	−0.005**	−0.005***	−0.005**	−0.004**	−0.004*
	Dummy for e-mail	0.074	0.074	0.160***	0.166**	0.129**	0.134**
Red tape, corruption and crime	Losses due to criminal activity (a)	−0.097***	−0.097***	−0.082****	−0.082****	−0.082****	−0.080***
	Manager's time spent in bur. issues (a)	−0.021***	−0.021**	−0.016**	−0.016*	−0.016**	−0.016*
	Illegal payments for protection	−0.254***	−0.254**	−0.205**	−0.216**	−0.229***	−0.238**
	Sales declared to taxes (a)	0.013***	0.013***	0.010***	0.010***	0.009***	0.009**
	Number of inspections	−0.032	−0.032	−0.027	−0.026	−0.028	−0.026
	Absenteeism (a)	−0.271**	−0.271**	−0.297**	−0.297**	−0.303**	−0.292**
	Dummy for lawsuit	−0.147***	−0.147***	−0.067	−0.069	−0.077*	−0.075
	Dummy for informal competition	−0.100**	−0.100**	−0.130***	−0.130***	−0.117***	−0.117**

Table 6c (cont.)

Blocks of IC variables	Explanatory ICA variables	Two-step estimation		Single-step estimation			
		Solow residual		Cobb-Douglas		Translog	
		OLS	RE	OLS	RE	OLS	RE
Finance and corporate governance	Dummy for external auditory (a)	0.769*	0.769**	1.008***	0.992***	0.800**	0.842**
Quality, innovation and labor skills	Dummy for new technology purchased (a)	0.187	0.187	0.256	0.26	0.295	0.318
	Staff-unskilled workers	−0.182**	−0.182**	−0.087	−0.079	−0.086	−0.081
	Staff-part time workers	−0.005***	−0.005***	−0.004**	−0.004**	−0.003	−0.003
	Weeks of training of skilled workers (a)	0.041***	0.041**	0.014	0.015	0.017	0.016
Other control variables	Age of the firm	−0.0001**	−0.0001	−0.0001	−0.0001	−0.0001	−0.0001
	Dummy for ownership	0.344**	0.344	0.447***	0.445*	0.453***	0.472**
	Dummy for small firms	−0.243***	−0.243***	−0.769***	−0.817***	−0.875***	−0.933***
	Dummy for médium	−0.289***	−0.289***	−0.435***	−0.467***	−0.546***	−0.585***
	N	1516	1516	1516	1516	1516	1516
	R^2	0.18	0.18	0.77	0.77	0.78	0.78

Notes: *significant at 10%; ** significant at 5%; *** significant at 1%. Each regression includes a set of industry dummies, year dummies and a constant term. (a) Variables instrumented with the industry-region-size average. RE: Random effects

Source: Escribano et al. (2008a) estimates with data from Turkey 2008 ES.

Table 6d de Loecker (2013) method and 2-steps using Solow residual based on Turkey 2008/2012/2018 ESs: Imputed samples

	2-step Restricted Solow res.	De Loecker (2013)
Electricity generator	−0.789***	−1.046***
	(0.196)	(0.174)
Losses due to criminal activity	−0.479***	−0.491***
	(0.063)	(0.154)
Security	−0.399	0.051
	(0.209)	(0.168)
Tax inspections	−0.0121	−0.0004
	(0.011)	(0.001)
Informal comp.	−0.187	−1.026***
	(0.183)	(0.159)
Bribes in taxes	−3.492**	−6.912***
	(1.057)	(1.589)
Equity financing	−0.00931***	0.01***
	(0.00176)	(0.002)
Sales after delivery	0.00045	−0.003***
	(0.00101)	(0.001)
Web page use	0.547*	0.375**
	(0.228)	(0.172)
Training	0.287	0.463***
	(0.268)	(0.166)
Age	−0.0375	−0.09***
	(0.0397)	(0.026)
N	1,112	489
R^2	0.14	0.62

Notes: *significant at 10%; ** significant at 5%; *** significant at 1%. Each regression includes a set of industry dummies, year dummies and a constant term.
Source: Authors' estimates with data from Turkey 2008, 2012 and 2018 ES.

$$\hat{\overline{tfp}}_t^d = \hat{\alpha}_1^{IC}\overline{IC}_1 + \ldots + \hat{\alpha}_r^{IC}\overline{IC}_r + \hat{\alpha}_C'\overline{C} + \hat{\alpha}_{Ds}'\overline{D}_j + \hat{\alpha}_{D2}'\overline{D}_t. \tag{27}$$

From (276) we can calculate the relative percentage contribution of each IC variable to the average of TFP from

$$100 = \frac{\hat{\alpha}_1^{IC}\overline{IC}_1 + \ldots + \hat{\alpha}_r^{IC}\overline{IC}_r + \hat{\alpha}_C'\overline{C} + \hat{\alpha}_{Ds}'\overline{D}_j + \hat{\alpha}_{D2}'\overline{D}_t}{\hat{\overline{tfp}}_t^d}100. \tag{28}$$

Table 7 Production function coefficients (elasticities) from the restricted estimations and results on the constant returns to scale (CRS) conditions

	Two-step Restricted Solow residual	One step-Restricted Cobb-Douglas	One-step Restricted Translog	Two-step LP	Two-step ACF
Employment	0.320	0.230	0.265	0.206	0.299
Materials	0.527	0.444	0.493	0.476	0.550
Capital	0.152	0.100	0.071	0.145	0.122
CRS	1.000	0.775	0.829	0.827	0.971

Source: Authors' estimates with data from Turkey 2018 ES.

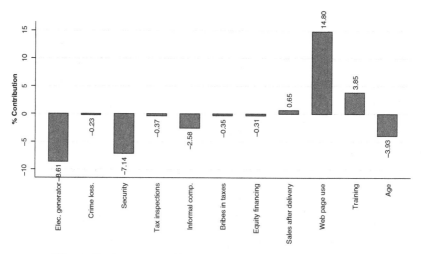

Figure 3a Average IC Effects on average TFP in Turkey 2018 ES

Note: The coefficients are those of the two-step specification using the restricted Solow residue as the dependent variable.

Source: Authors' estimates with data from Turkey 2018 ES.

The results of equation (28) using the samples of Turkey from 2018 and 2008 are shown in Figures (3a) and (3b)

To compensate the problem where some IC variables have positive effects and other IC variables have negative effects (small IC net effect), in order to assess the magnitude or the overall importance of the IC we add all the individual averages of IC contributions in absolute value. That is, from equation (28) we get that

Table 8 Production function coefficients (elasticities) from the unrestricted estimations and results on the constant returns to scale (CRS) conditions

		Food	Textiles	Garments	Metal Prods.	Mach. & Equipment	Other Manuf.
Two-step Unrestricted Solow residual	Empl.	0.315	0.303	0.352	0.308	0.313	0.327
	Materials	0.539	0.553	0.521	0.504	0.510	0.530
	Capital	0.146	0.144	0.127	0.189	0.177	0.143
	CRS	1.000	1.000	1.000	1.000	1.000	1.000
One-step Unrestricted Cobb-Douglas	Empl.	0.160	0.237	0.187	0.407	0.108	0.340
	Materials	0.668	0.306	0.554	0.374	0.422	0.360
	Capital	0.041	0.091	0.098	0.071	0.155	0.080
	CRS	0.870	0.634	0.838	0.852	0.684	0.780
One-step Unrestricted Translog	Empl.	0.247	0.238	0.182	0.466	0.310	0.359
	Materials	0.610	0.460	0.614	0.417	0.353	0.406
	Capital	0.034	0.039	0.057	0.053	0.096	0.049
	CRS	0.890	0.737	0.853	0.936	0.760	0.814

Source: Authors' estimates with data from Turkey 2018 ES.

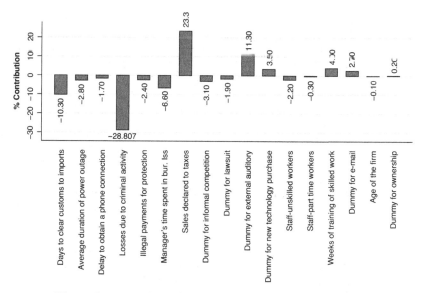

Figure 3b Average IC effects on average TFP in Turkey 2008 ES
Source: Escribano et al. (2008a) estimates with data from Turkey 2008 ES.

$$\left|\widehat{tfp_t^d}\right| \leq \overline{\left|\widehat{tfp_t^d}\right|} \triangleq \left|\hat{\alpha}_1^{IC}\overline{IC}_1\right| + \ldots + \left|\hat{\alpha}_1^{IC}\overline{IC}_r\right| + \left|\hat{\alpha}_C'\overline{C}\right| + \left|\hat{\alpha}_{Ds}'\overline{D}_j\right|$$
$$+ \left|\hat{\alpha}_{Ds}'\overline{D}_t\right| + + \left|\overline{\hat{e}}_t\right| \tag{29}$$

which expressed in percentage terms is

$$100 = \frac{\left|\hat{\alpha}_1^{IC}\overline{IC}_1\right| + \ldots + \left|\hat{\alpha}_r^{IC}\overline{IC}_r\right| + \left|\hat{\alpha}_C'\overline{C}\right|}{\left|\widehat{tfp_t^d}\right|} 100$$
$$+ \frac{\left|\hat{\alpha}_{D2}'\overline{D}_j\right| + \left|\hat{\alpha}_{D2}'\overline{D}_t\right| + \left|\overline{\hat{e}}_t\right|}{\left|\widehat{tfp_t^d}\right|} 100. \tag{30}$$

To compare the relative absolute contribution of each block of IC variables to the total of the TFP associated only with the IC variables, we calculated the following percentage in absolute value of IC, relative to the concept of absolute TFP value associated to IC variables only, eliminating the contributions of the other variables (D_j, D_t) from the second expression of equation (29), to get

$$\overline{\left|\widehat{tfp_t^{IC}}\right|} = \left|\hat{\alpha}_1^{IC}\overline{IC}_1\right| + \ldots + \left|\hat{\alpha}_r^{IC}\overline{IC}_r\right| + \left|\hat{\alpha}_C'\overline{C}\right| \tag{31}$$

and therefore equation (29) is reduced to equation (31),

$$100 = \frac{|\hat{\alpha}_I^{IC}\overline{IC_1}| + \ldots + |\hat{\alpha}_r^{IC}\overline{IC_r}| + |\hat{\alpha}_C'\overline{C}|}{|\hat{tfp}^{IC}|} 100. \tag{32}$$

The concept of total factor productivity that allows us to make international comparisons of productivity (TFP), avoiding the problem of comparing apples with oranges, is TFP^{IC} (or in logs TFP^{IC}). That is, the part of TFP that is only associated with the IC and the other control economic variables (C). To do this, we eliminate from equation (26) the components associated with (D$_j$, D$_t$) so that

$$\hat{tfp}_{it}^{IC} = \hat{tfp}_{it}^d - \hat{\alpha}_{Ds}'D_j - \hat{\alpha}_{D2}'D_t - \hat{e}_{it} = \hat{\alpha}_{IC}'IC_{it} + \hat{\alpha}_C'C_{it} \tag{33}$$

is the estimated TFP associated with the IC and C variables (named TFP^{IC}). Instead of directly comparing the TFP among countries, we compare the impacts that the IC has on the TFP of those countries by comparing estimates of TFP^{IC}, as we will see in the empirical applications.

4.3 Beyond Marginal Effects: Assessing the IC Effects on Aggregate TFP^{IC}

In this section, from a neoclassical perspective, we propose to use the decomposition of Olley and Pakes (1996) as an aggregation mechanism of the individual behavior described in equation (34), so that we can use the *aggregate* TFP as a reference point for further evaluations of the IC. Let the aggregate (or weighted) productivity be defined as[26]

$$TFP_t = \sum_{i=1}^{N} s_{it}TFP_{it}, \tag{34}$$

obtained as the weighted average of the productivities at company level ($TFP_{it} = exp(TFP_{it})$), where N *is* the number of companies in the analyzed sample. The weights (s_{it}) indicate the proportion of the sales of company i over the total sales (Y) of sector j in that year $\left(s_{it} = Y_{it}/\sum_{i=1}^{N}Y_{it}\right)$. This is $\overline{TFP}_t = N^{-1}\sum_{i=1}^{N}TFP_{it}$ the average productivity of the companies in the sample. The aggregate productivity can then be decomposed as

---

[26] Similar aggregate productivity expressions as equation (25), and also similar decompositions introduced in this section of the Element, can be obtained at the *aggregate level of the industry*, or at the *aggregate level of the region*, by considering in equation (25) only those productivity values and the share of sales of the firms of certain industries or certain regions.

$$TFP_t = \overline{TFP_t} + \sum_{i=1}^{N} \tilde{s}_{it} \widetilde{TFP}_{it}, \tag{35}$$

where $\tilde{s}_{it} = (s_{it} - \bar{s}_t)$ and when $\widetilde{TFP}_{it} = (TFP_{it} - \overline{TFP_t})$ they are in the deviations from the mean.

The first term of equation (35) is the *average productivity* and the second term measures the *efficiency* or covariance between each company's share of sales and its productivity, $\hat{cov}(s_{it}, TFP_{it})$, multiplied by the number of companies (N). If the covariance is positive, then the greater the covariance, the greater the share of sales that the most productive firms will have. Therefore, if allocation efficiency increases, aggregate productivity will improve. However, if the covariance is negative, there are inefficiencies in resource allocation and the more negative the covariance, the greater the share of output going to less productive firms, reducing aggregate productivity.

Similarly we can calculate the aggregate productivity but for TFP measured in logarithms

$$tfp_t = \sum_{i=1}^{N} s_{it} tfp_{it} \tag{36}$$

then the *Mixed O&P Decomposition* on logTFP = TFP becomes

$$tfp_t = \overline{tfp_t} + \sum_{i=1}^{N} \tilde{s}_{it} \widetilde{tfp}_{it}, \tag{37}$$

where $\tilde{s}_{it} = (s_{it} - \bar{s}_t)$ and $\widetilde{tfp}_{it} = (tfp_{it} - \overline{tfp_t})$ are at deviations from the average.

The first term is the average *logarithmic* productivity $\left(\overline{tfp_t} = N^{-1} \sum_{i=1}^{N} tfp_{it} \right)$ while the second measures the *allocative efficiency* among the variables.

In order to make international TFP comparisons among countries, avoiding the problem of comparing apples and oranges, it is convenient to create an index of TFP associated with the IC (named TFP^{IC}). The useful additive property of equations (36) and (37), when considering TFP instead of TFP^{IC} directly, allows us to obtain an accurate solution in closed form to the decomposition of aggregate logarithmic TFP and the IC variables. After subtracting the constant, industry dummies, regional dummies and time dummies from log-productivity (TFP) at the enterprise level, we concentrate on the estimated part of the TFP exclusively associated with the IC and other control variables. Thus, from equation (25) we get,

$$tfp_{it}^{IC} = tfp_{it}^{d} - \hat{a}_P - \hat{a}_{Ds}'D_j - \hat{a}_{D2}'D_t - \hat{e}_{it} = \hat{a}_{IC}'IC_{it} + \hat{a}_C'C_{it}, \qquad (38)$$

where the set of estimated parameters used comes from the *TFP estimate*. In the next step we can add the individual behaviors associated with the IC and C variables to calculate the following O&P decomposition of TFP^{IC}, where $tfp_t^{IC} = \sum_{i=1}^{N} s_{it} tfp_{it}^{IC}$ and therefore,

$$tfp_t^{IC} = \overline{tfp_t^{IC}} + N\hat{c}ov(s_{it}, tfp_{it}^{IC}). \qquad (39)$$

Similarly, with the TFP in levels associated with the IC and C variables:
$$TFP_{it}^{IC} = \exp(\hat{a}_{IC}'IC_{it} + \hat{a}_C'C_{it})$$

$$TFP_t^{IC} = \overline{TFP_t^{IC}} + N\,\hat{c}ov(s_{it}, TFP_{it}^{IC}) \qquad (40)$$

Equation (29) is of particular interest since it allows us to directly exploit the additive property of expression (17) to evaluate the relative contributions of the IC to *TFP*. To do the same from expression (30), we would need to make simulations of changes in the IC variables to evaluate their impact (see Escribano, Guasch and Pena, 2019). From now on we will concentrate on the analysis of the components of equation (40), which, because it is additive, therefore allows us to evaluate the contribution of each IC variable to the aggregate TFP (tfp_t^{IC}) by means of equation (41),

$$tfp_t^{IC} = \overline{\hat{a}}_{IC}'\overline{IC}_t + \overline{\hat{a}}_{IC}'\overline{C}_t + N\hat{a}_{IC}'\,\hat{c}ov(s_{it}, IC_{it}) + N\hat{a}_C'\,\hat{c}ov(s_{it}, C_{it}). \qquad (41)$$

From equation (40), in percent, we get that

$$100 = \frac{100}{tfp_t^{IC}}[\overline{\hat{a}}_{IC}'\,\overline{IC}_t + \overline{\hat{a}}_C'\,\overline{C}_t + N\hat{a}_{IC}'\,\hat{c}ov(s_{it}, IC_{it}) + N\hat{a}_C'\,\hat{c}ov(s_{it}, C_{it})].$$

$$(42)$$

The use of equation (42) has several advantages since it allows us to make direct comparisons of the percentage contributions of the IC and C economic variables over the aggregate TFP^{IC} as the sum of the impact on the mean TFP^{IC} and the allocative efficiency terms of each IC and C variable.

The overall aggregate effect of the IC variables, IC_{it} and C_{it}, on aggregate TFP is driven by two factors: its (i) *"contribution to the average TFP"* and (ii) the *"contribution of the inter-enterprise resource allocation component."* Therefore, we can now go beyond the assessment of pure marginal economic effects (elasticities and semi-elasticities) given by the coefficients $\hat{a}_{IC}'$. The importance of using each firm's market share as a TFP aggregation mechanism in the decomposition of O&P is because we would like to have a high proportion of resources in the hands of highly productive firms. If we use the same argument with the IC variables, we would like not to have the IC constraints affecting most productive companies with high market shares, because the impact on the whole economy would be very large. Similarly, the positive effects of the IC should be concentrated on the most productive companies with high market shares in order to derive maximum social benefit from their positive social effect on *TFP*. Formally, let us write equation (39) as

$$tfp_t^{IC} = \hat{a}_{IC,1}\overline{IC_{1t}} + N\hat{a}_{IC,1}\ \hat{c}ov(s_{it}, IC_{i1t}) + \ldots + \hat{a}_{IC,J}\overline{IC_{iJt}}$$
$$+ N\hat{a}_{IC,J}\hat{c}ov(s_{it}, IC_{iJt}) + \hat{a}_C'\overline{C_t} + N\hat{a}_C'\hat{c}ov(s_{it}, C_{it}) \tag{43}$$

Therefore in equation (43), the *aggregate* TFP associated with the IC and C economic variables is the sum of the contributions of each IC and C variable to the *mean* TFP and of the contribution of each IC and C variable to the *allocative* efficiency (covariances).

The *contribution to the average is* directly interpreted as the contribution of the IC of a representative company/firm if they were all equally productive (equal TFP) and there was no correlation between the market share of sales and the IC and C variables.

Allocative efficiency indicates how the IC effects are redistributed across firms on the TFP depending on their market shares. In Table 9, we distinguish the four possible cases of resource reallocation. Consider a variable with a negative IC effect on the TFP (i.e., a counter-productive IC variable): if the covariance with their market share is negative, this indicates that those companies suffering from the IC restriction are also those with low sale's market shares. Therefore, these firms use a low proportion of the resources and the negative *average contribution* will be to some extent cushioned by the allocative efficiency component since it is multiplied by a negative IC coefficient; see equation (43) and Table 9.

Table 9 Summary of IC contributions to the allocative efficiency term

		Covariance term or allocative efficiency	
		$\hat{c}ov(s_{it}, IC_{iJt}) > 0$	$\hat{c}ov(s_{it}, IC_{iJt}) < 0$
IC Effect on *TFP*	$\hat{a}_{IC,J} > 0$	Overall allocative effect > 0	Overall allocative effect < 0
	$\hat{a}_{IC,J} < 0$	Overall allocative effect < 0	Overall allocative effect > 0

Note: The overall allocative effect of the IC variable J is given by $N\hat{a}_{IC,J}\ \hat{c}ov(s_{it}, IC_{iJt})$.

From an institutional perspective, we do not want the TFP of resource-intensive companies to be greatly affected by IC constraints, or barriers, as it will seriously affect the entire economy. Similarly, we want the pro-productive IC variables to be concentrated on highly productive firms with high market shares to amplify the positive effect on the average TFP, reflected by a positive covariance (reallocation); the economy uses its resources more efficiently. On the other hand, when the positive effect of the IC is concentrated on firms with low shares of sales and low productivity, the economy is not getting the maximum benefit from the IC variable in terms of *aggregate* TFP, since the positive effect of the IC variable is mainly enjoyed by firms with low shares of sales.

These arguments, in favor of the most productive companies gaining market share, have to be accompanied by significant competition policy controls to avoid abuse of a dominant position of large incumbent companies. Firms with greater market shares would try to impose entry barriers on new firms or on recent entrants.

4.4 Empirical results of the contributions of the IC on the O&P decomposition

We begin this subsection by introducing the *mixed Olley-Pakes TFP decomposition* of equation (36). For that, in Figures 4 and 5 we calculate this mixed TFP decomposition by region and by industry of the manufacturing sector for the Turkey 2018 ES.[27]

According to this static picture of the efficiency of manufacturing industry, by region (Figure 4) the South-East Anatolia and Mediterranean regions are the most productive, partly because the average company in these regions is slightly more productive than its counterpart in other regions. In addition, the positive and higher estimated allocative efficiency effect also contributes to the higher estimated aggregate logarithmic TFP in these two regions. In other words, in these two regions resources tend to be concentrated in firms that, while having higher market share, are also efficient firms in terms of TFP. The other two regions having large and positive allocative efficiency terms are Northest Anatolia and East Black Sea Region.

In Figure 5, by focusing on the mixed of O&P decompositions by sector, we are able to address some key differences on aggregate TFP and its components. In this case, there is one sector where the aggregate TFP is significantly higher

---

[27] We concentrate only on the mixed O&P decomposition. However, the conclusions we want to address here are robust to the use of the O&P decomposition in levels of TFP; see Escribano at al. (2008a, 2008b).

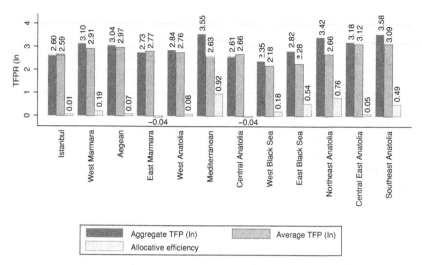

Figure 4 O&P mixed decomposition by region based on Turkey 2018 ES

Notes: Mixed TFP decomposition of O&P calculated according to equation (36). The TFP measure used is the Solow restricted residuals in logs; 2% of the upper and lower limits of productivity in each region is excluded from the calculations.

Source: Authors' estimates with data from Turkey 2018 ES.

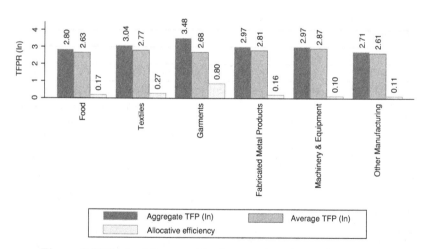

Figure 5 O&P mixed decomposition by sector based on Turkey 2018 ES

Notes: The O&P mixed decomposition by industry/sector according to equation (36). The productivity measure used is the Solow restricted waste in levels; 2% of the upper and lower TFP values for each sector excluded from the calculations.

Source: Authors' estimates with data from Turkey 2018 ES.

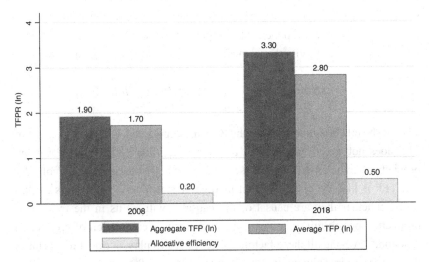

Figure 6 O&P mixed TFP decomposition in 2008 and 2018

Notes: The O&P mixed annual TFP decomposition according to equation (36). The TFP measure used is the Solow restricted residuals in levels; 2% of the upper and lower TFP values for each sector excluded from the calculations.

Source: Authors' estimates with data from Turkey 2008 ES and Turkey 2018 ES.

than the rest; "Garments." In this sector, it is the positive allocative efficiency term (0.80) that is making its aggregate TFP stand out over other sectors.

Continuing with Figure 6, which shows the mixed OP decomposition for the whole country in 2008 and 2018, it is also noteworthy that, for the whole country, the aggregate log TFP is 9.5 times higher than the allocative efficiency component in 2008 and 6.5 higher in 2019; therefore, the relative importance of the allocative efficiency component has increased between 2008 and 2018 in Turkey and all the TFP components have also increased between 2008 and 2018. This means that aggregate logarithmic productivity in Turkey is mainly driven by the TFP of the average company (establishment) and only marginally by the allocative efficiency term although the contribution of this last term is increasing through time. Finally, Figure 6 shows the evolution of the aggregated TFP between 2008 and 2018. A remarkable growth of TFP is observed in the period, and this increase is driven by the two terms of the mixed O&P decomposition. The average component grows from 1.7 to 2.8, while the allocation component grows from 0.2 to 0.5.

These are key findings in the case of Turkey that will impact on the analysis in the following sections. A large allocative efficiency effect implies a better allocation of resources toward the most productive firms, but also a large difference between low- and high-productivity firms. In other words, there is scope for reallocating resources and/or bringing low-productivity firms closer to the most successful firms. This is important in terms of potential productivity gains from the perspective of economic policies that soften the constraints on the IC. In what follows, we aim to identify the IC factors that have contributed to this increase.

How Important Is the IC for Aggregate TFP? Introduction to the Important Concept of TFP^{IC}

What is the relative importance of the IC in the aggregated TFP? Our measure of TFP does not exactly correspond to the true technical efficiency of a given productive sector, as will be discussed in Section 5. On the contrary, we consider that TFP is like the black-box that incorporates all those multifactors associated – whether they are causal or not causal – with shifts in the frontier of production possibilities or toward the pure factor accumulation of production function.[28] Among all these factors the IC variables play a critical role. This is the purpose of introducing the IC concept of TFP, TFP^{IC}.

In Figure 7, if we normalize the aggregate TFP to a value of 100, according to our estimates, 35.8 percent is associated with the investment climate (IC and C)

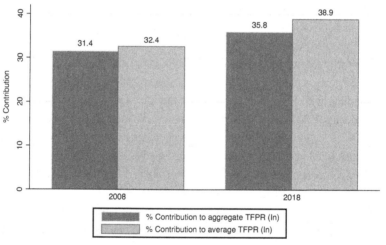

Figure 7 Proportion of the IC on aggregate TFP^{IC} and average TFP^{IC}

Notes: From equations (26) and (33), the proportion of the IC effects on TFP relative to aggregate TFP^{IC} on aggregate TFP^d and average TFP^{IC} on average TFP^d can be computed as the ratios of aggregate TFP^{IC} to aggregate TFP^d of average TFP^{IC} to average TFP^d.

Source: Authors' estimates with data from Turkey 2018 ES.

---

[28] Identifying TFP with technical efficiency is not possible unless some restrictive assumptions are made. We do not want to include additional assumptions in the models, so we prefer to avoid interpreting TFP as technical efficiency.

and the remaining 64.2 percent is associated with other factors affecting the firms but that are not included as part of the IC. Two good surveys on factors empirically associated with the TFP in the literature are Bartelsman and Doms (2000) and Ahn (2001).

Consider that only the average IC and C effects on average TFP in 2018 is 38.9 percent. However, when aggregating the firm level effects with the shares of the IC impact, then aggregate TFP is reduced from 38.9 to 35.9 percent. This is due to the positive effect of the allocative efficiency component of the TFP^{IC}. This effect is also observed in 2008. The explanation for this phenomenon lies in the distribution of the positive and negative IC effects on TFP among Turkish companies according to their market share. In Table 6a–d we already explained the possible effects of the IC coefficients on the allocation of resources. Companies having a positive IC effects on TFP tend are usually companies with high market shares, and conversely, IC variables with negative effects tend to be concentrated on companies with low market shares.

4.5 International Comparisons of IC Conditions Based on TFP^{IC}

A better understanding of the role of the IC on TFP is obtained by applying the mixed O&P decomposition to the concept of TFP^{IC}. Remember that we have defined TFP^{IC} as the part of the TFP that is exclusively associated with the investment climate (IC and C variables). Figure 8 makes an international comparison of the mixed O&P decompositions of TFP^{IC} for Turkey and for other selected emerging countries.

The aggregate TFP of the Turkish manufacturing industry is, in general, negatively influenced (constrained) by the IC. Numerically, year 2008 was at a level similar to Indonesia and the Philippines, and was considerably lower than in other countries such as South Africa, Brazil or especially Chile, where better IC conditions stimulate companies to use the economy's resources more efficiently, in that the IC has a positive effect on TFP^{IC}. However, in Turkey there was a considerable improvement in investment conditions between 2008 and 2018, with the aggregate TFP^{IC} going from –0.58 to –0.13.

What is the role of the two O&P components of the TFP^{IC} in this improve-ment? The average component went from –0.7 to –0.14, while the efficiency component went from 0.12 to 0.01. In other words, the improvement in the conditions of the IC in Turkey comes from the average effect alone, with a small worsening of the allocative efficiency effect. The interpretation is that for the average Turkish company, the IC conditions have improved. Also, the alloca-tion of resources has become more equitable over the period. The value of 0.12 observed in 2008 indicates that to a large extent the positive IC conditions are

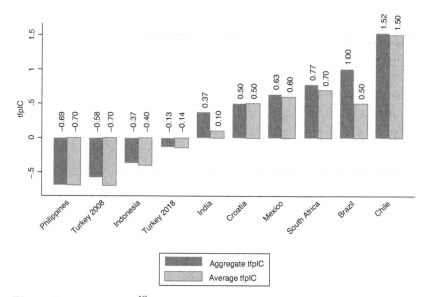

Figure 8 O&P mixed TFP^{IC} decomposition of Turkey and selected emerging countries

Notes: Mixed O&P are decomposed according to equation (43) based on the Solow residuals.

Source: Authors' estimates with data from Turkey 2018 ES and other ESs from selected emerging countries.

concentrated in companies with a high market share, while in 2018 the effects were much more balanced.

In 2008, the Turkish economy was much more dual, with large companies enjoying relatively good IC conditions in terms of corruption, crime, infrastructure, etc., while the negative IC effects of these variables were concentrated in small companies in terms of sales. This generated a significant bottleneck for new businesses to enter. In the last decade, this effect has been corrected, which favors the entry of new competitors and the probability of their survival, improving in turn the competitiveness of the economy.

On the other hand, the observed values of the TFP^{IC} do not imply that Turkey is less productive than other countries, but rather that the effect of the IC on TFP in Turkey is less than in other countries and that the negative factors of the IC dominate over the positive factors. A plausible and intuitive economic interpretation is that the TFP^{IC} may indicate that the IC available for doing business is preventing the economy from using its resources as efficiently as possible.

Similarly to the case of regular O&P decomposition of TFP, the dominant component of decomposition is again the average TFP^{IC}. In particular for

Turkey, 99 percent of the aggregate TFP^{IC} is due to the average TFP^{IC} component, while the remaining 1 percent is due to the allocative efficient effect. As long as the overall effect of the IC is negative, we can say that the average company in Turkey faces a restrictive business environment, and this effect is directly transmitted to the aggregate TFP^{IC}. However, the allocation component is positive although it is less than in other countries. In other words, as the positive effects of IC tend to be concentrated on firms with a high market share and the negative effects on firms with a low market share, the negative contribution to the average TFP^{IC} is slightly cushioned. These results are important because, as we will see in the next sections, they suggest channels through which Turkish productivity could be increased.

From the previous subsections we know that the IC plays an important role in Turkey's productivity. The objective now is to identify the main individual contributors of the IC to the effect of the IC defined so far. In particular, there are two issues that we want to address here; first, the relevance of the IC effect (how many companies are affected by the IC constraints. For example, how many companies suffer from power cuts, so that firms need an electricity generator, and how many power cuts do they suffer from. Second, which companies are predominantly affected by the problem. The latter is particularly important because a positive effect of the IC concentrated on firms with a high market share amplifies the original effect, since it is concentrated on the firms that use most of the economy's resources. By having a better IC, the firms become more productive and they can get a higher return using the same amount of inputs, which translates into an increase in the general welfare of the economy as a whole, in that the economy is using its resources more efficiently. The same goes for the negative aspects of the IC, because if they are concentrated in companies with high market shares the negative IC impact is amplified exponentially. In summary, the contribution of the IC to aggregate TFP can be decomposed into the accumulation effect[29] (average productivity) and the distributive effect[30] (allocative efficiency).

Analysis of the Absolute Effects of the IC by Groups of Variables

A good starting point in the analysis of the individual IC contributions to the TFP^{IC} is given in Figure 9, which shows the relative importance of each group

---

[29] We say that the average company is suffering a certain number of power outages, spends a certain number of hours dealing with bureaucracy and tax inspections, suffers losses due to criminal activity and reports bribes as a certain percentage of sales to taxes, etc. In other words, we evaluate the IC effect on the TFP of the average (or representative) company.

[30] What we take into account now is the way in which the IC variable is distributed among companies according to their share of sales.

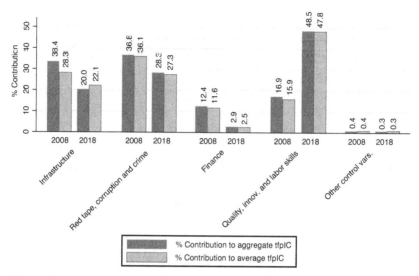

Figure 9 Absolute percentage contribution of the IC by blocks of variables to the mixed O&P decomposition of TFP^{IC}

Notes: Mixed O&P decomposition of TFP^{IC} from equation (32). The TFP measure used is the restricted Solow residual.

Source: Authors' estimates with data from Turkey 2018 ES.

of IC variables obtained from Turkey 2008 ES and Turkey 2018 ES. In that figure, to avoid the compensating effect of having positive and negative IC effects on TFP, we take the IC contributions in absolute value. Almost 78 percent of the TFP^{IC} is represented by three groups of IC variables: (i) infrastructure; (ii) red tape, corruption and crime; and (iii) quality, innovation and labor skills. The weight of the infrastructure group went down from 2008 to 2018 from 30 percent to 20 percent of TFP^{IC}, respectively. The second group of red tape, corruption and crime maintains the percentage in both years at around 30 percent. The third group of quality, innovation and labor skills increases a lot from 2008 to 2018, from 8 percent to 48 percent of TFP^{IC}, respectively. The finance group has only a marginal weight on TFP^{IC}.

As for the contributions of the different IC groups, there are no major differences between the aggregated TFP^{IC} and the average TFP^{IC}. When the contribution to allocative efficiency of a given group is lower than the contribution to the average, we say that the group effect – positive or negative – is reduced by concentrating on firms with a low market share. This is what happens with the infrastructure group of Figure 9 in 2018, which goes from 22.1 to 20 percent and there is a negative allocative efficiency effect, although relatively it is not very important. The reduced contribution of the allocative efficiency effect is consistent with what was observed in Figure 8 where we saw that the average TFP^{IC} component dominated aggregate TFP^{IC}.

The comparison between 2008 and 2018 is interesting. The group quality, innovation and labor skills gains a lot of importance, going from 8.3 to 48.5. Finance and "Other Control Variables" lose importance from 9.7 to 2.9 percent and 23.9 to 0.3 percent, respectively. The infrastructure group drops slightly from 29.2 to 20 percent, while the red tape, corruption and crime group maintains its contribution at around 29 percent.

Analysis of the Individual Effects of IC on the Components of the O&P Decomposition of the TFP^{IC}

In the case of Turkey, the effect of the individual IC variables is transmitted to the aggregate TFP through the average TFP and, to a lesser extent, through the IC effect of the allocative efficiency term (but not on the IC effect on the market shares).[31] This means that the IC effect on aggregate is equal to 100 percent, 85 percent of which is due to the effect on average TFP and the remaining 15 percent is due to the effect on the allocative efficiency term.

From a general perspective we can get, from Figure 10, some basic conclusions that can help us explain why the overall climate effect of investment is limiting the aggregate TFP of the Turkish manufacturing sector. All the statistically significant variables within the infrastructure and red tape, corruption and crime groups have a negative effect (constraints) on TFP. This is one of the reasons for the negative decrease in the estimated aggregate TFP^{IC}. However, the variables in the quality innovation and labor skills group have positive effects and cushion the IC negative effect of the other variables.

In the following, we describe the main individual contributors of the IC to the decline in TFP^{IC}. Notice that, for simplicity, we do not include the IC contributions of the IC to the allocative efficiency term in Figure 10, as those can easily be obtained as the contributions to the aggregate TFP^{IC} minus the corresponding contributions to the average TFP^{IC}. The following main five empirical results are drawn from Figure 10.

Web page use (quality, innovation and labor skills IC group). This variable is the largest contributor to aggregate productivity, with a 13.26 percent contribution. The average contribution is practically the same at 13.13 percent. Therefore, Web page use is widespread in Turkey, with no differences between companies with different market shares.

---

[31] We cannot directly address what is the actual effect of the IC on the allocative efficiency, since we are only analyzing the IC in the TFP but not in the market shares of sales of each firm.

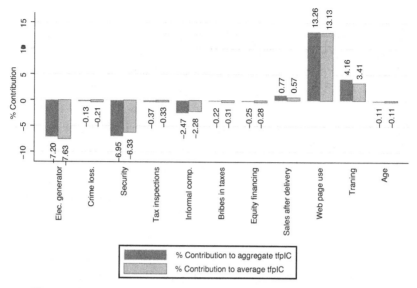

Figure 10 Percentage IC contributions of the aggregate and average TFP^{IC}

Notes: Contributions calculated according to equation (43). The TFP^{IC} measure used is from the Solow restricted residuals; 2% of the upper and lower values of TFP are excluded from the calculations.

Source: Authors' calculations with data from Turkey 2018 ES.

Electricity generator (infrastructure IC group). This variable is related to the quality of the energy infrastructure. If many companies have to invest in this type of alternative generator, it is because the public electricity infrastructure is deficient. This variable represents –7.2 percent of the aggregate TFP^{IC} and there are no important differences in the allocative efficiency effect.

Security (red tape, corruption and crime IC group). The fact that a significant proportion of companies in the same region and sector have to invest in security reveals a problem of criminality. This variable represents –6.95 percent; the average TFP^{IC} component is –6.3 percent, which tends to affect more companies with small market shares.

Training (quality, innovation and labor skills IC group). The other variable in the innovation and labor skills group contributes 4.2 percent to aggregate TFP^{IC}. The average TFP^{IC} contribution is 3.4, and tends to be concentrated in companies with a high market shares.

Informal competition (red tape, corruption and crime IC group). This variable represents a bottleneck for aggregate TFP^{IC}, its contribution is –2.5 percent and this affects all companies equally.

The remaining IC variables all have very small TFP contributions at below 0.4 percent. It is noteworthy that most of the significant variables are in the IC block of red tape, corruption and crime, which indicates that the main bottlenecks for improvements in productivity in Turkey in 2008 are still present in 2018.

4.6 Relationship between TFP^{IC} and Other Indexes of a Country's Economic Situation: Income Per-Capita, Doing Business and Global Competitive Index

The results of Figure 8 indicate a negative effect of the IC on the aggregated TFP^{IC} in Turkey 2008 ES and Turkey 2018 ES and the effect of the IC in Turkey shows an atypical behavior when compared to other countries with similar levels of per capita income. Figure 11 shows the cross-plot between per capita GDP and TFP^{IC}, the measure of the IC effects on aggregate TFP for the manufacturing sector of thirty-nine countries. For all thirty-nine countries, we

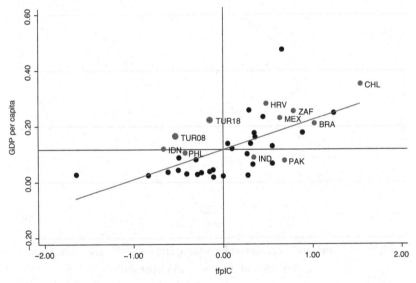

Figure 11 International cross-plot between aggregate TFP^{IC} and GDP per capita

Sample of 39 countries: Algeria, Bangladesh, Bolivia, Botswana, Brazil, Burkina Faso, Cameroon, Chile, Colombia, Costa Rica, Croatia, Ecuador, Egypt, El Salvador, Eritrea, Ethiopia, Honduras, India, Indonesia, Kenya, Madagascar, Malawi, Mali, Mauritania, Mauritius, Mexico, Morocco, Namibia, Nicaragua, Niger, Pakistan, Philippines, Senegal, South Africa, Swaziland, Tanzania, Turkey, Uganda, Zambia

Source: Staff calculations with various ICS data and Penn World Table data.

applied the same TFP methodology described in this Element, as initially suggested by Escribano and Guasch (2004, 2005). From Figure 11 we can identify a large gap between the position that Turkey occupies in GPD per capita (a level similar to those in Mexico or Brazil) and the position it should occupy in terms of TFP^{IC} (with countries having negative values of TFP^{IC}). Therefore, a key factor in the lack of convergence of the Turkish economy can be found in the negative role (constraints) the IC has on the competitiveness and productivity of Turkish enterprises. Notice, however, that there was an appreciable IC improvement TFP^{IC}, from 2008 to 2018, bringing Turkey a bit closer to the level of similar emerging countries in terms of per capita GDP.

For example, Figure 12 shows the cross-plot between the IC contribution on TFP^{IC} of the IC block or variables from innovation and labor skills group and TFP^{IC}. This international correlation, between this IC block of the thirty-nine countries and their corresponding TFP^{IC} values, is positive and very high. There

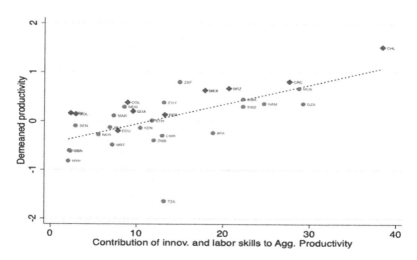

Figure 12 International cross-plot between aggregate TFP^{IC} and the IC block contribution of innovation and labor skills

Sample of 39 countries: Algeria, Bangladesh, Bolivia, Botswana, Brazil, Burkina Faso, Cameroon, Chile, Colombia, Costa Rica, Croatia, Ecuador, Egypt, El Salvador, Eritrea, Ethiopia, Honduras, India, Indonesia, Kenya, Madagascar, Malawi, Mali, Mauritania, Mauritius, Mexico, Morocco, Namibia, Nicaragua, Niger, Pakistan, Philippines, Senegal, South Africa, Swaziland, Tanzania, Turkey, Uganda, Zambia

Source: Staff calculations with various ICS data and Penn World Table data.

is unanimous consensus in society globally that improving process-innovation and product-innovation will enhance productivity and therefore improve the competitive environment in which firms operate. A key instrument for that is to increase the *absorptive capacity* of the firm, as was theoretically suggested by Cohen and Levinthal (1989, 1990) and its relevance demonstrated empirically by Escribano, Fosfuri and Tribo (2009). Key elements to improve the absorptive capacity measure (formed by the main principal components) at the firm level, are the amount of investment in R&D within the firm, R&D skills, the fact that firms have permanent R&D departments and the continuity of the training programs of their workers. In particular, in Turkey, two of the key elements within this group of IC variables are the *use of Web pages* and the *training of their workers*; see Figure 3a.

Organizations with higher levels of absorptive capacity manage external knowledge flows more efficiently and stimulate innovation. The absorptive capacity of the firm is the ability to recognize the value of new external knowledge, assimilate this value for the firm and use such knowledge.

The impact of that knowledge on absorptive capacity depends on the business environment where the companies operate and on the quality of the institutions ("rule of law" and "rules of the game") available in each country. For that purpose, the descriptive information coming from the Doing Business reports of the World Bank is very useful. In particular, we aim to know the relation with our econometric analysis on the IC impact on TFP (TFP^{IC}).

Table 10 presents information on selected indicators from the Doing Business Report (2018) of emerging countries competing with Turkey: Brazil, Chile, China, India and Mexico. However, for Turkey we give the values for years 2008 and 2018. The higher the value on the ease of doing business, the worse is the relative situation of the country in the ranking. Turkey's firms in 2008 were close to the middle rank position (62 out of 178 countries) on the ease of doing business. Those elements with scores higher than the average (62 in 2008 and 71 in 2018) indicate the main constraints for doing business. From Table 10, we see in bold numbers that in 2018 Turkey's performance was similar to that of Chile or Mexico but worse than Brazil, China and India in terms of the ease of doing business. The main bad individual elements for doing business, common to both years (2008 and 2018) in Turkey, are starting a business, registering a property, paying taxes and trading across borders and in 2018 also getting electricity. It is noteworthy that this picture is similar to what we obtained as main constraints from the econometric analysis of Figure 3a where we identify electricity problems (i.e., it is necessary to have electricity generators) and problems

Table 10 International scores in the Doing Business Reports

Economic Index	Brazil (2018)	Chile (2018)	China (2018)	India (2018)	Mexico (2018)	Turkey (2018)	Turkey (2008)
Ease of doing business score	55.6	72	65.2	60.9	72.5	70.9	61.6
Score-Starting a business	64.8	87.2	85.4	73.9	85.8	81.9	80.5
Score-Dealing with construction permits	52.1	75.8	41.2	39.7	67.8	69.6	40
Score-Getting electricity	70.8	85.7	65.7	88.6	71	81	0
Score-Registering property	52.6	71.1	75	46.1	60.8	81.5	75.6
Score-Getting a loan	45	55	60	75	90	55	56.3
Score-Protecting minority investors	62	66	56	80	62	76	53.3
Score-Paying taxes	34.4	75.8	63.3	65.2	66.5	73.1	78.4
Score-Trading across borders	63	80.6	70.7	58.6	82.1	87.9	69.5
Score-Enforcing contracts	64.1	62.8	79	41.2	67	69.9	64.1
Score-Resolving insolvency	47.5	59.5	55.8	40.7	72.3	33.3	35.5

Source: World Bank, 2020.

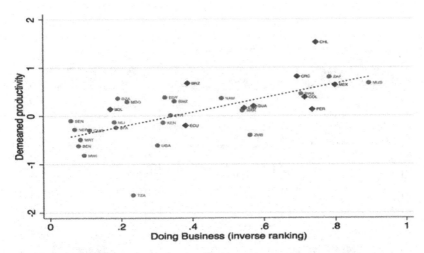

Figure 13 Cross-plot between the TFP^{IC} aggregate and the ranking (inverse) in the Doing Business Report

Sample of 39 countries: Algeria, Bangladesh, Bolivia, Botswana, Brazil, Burkina Faso, Cameroon, Chile, Colombia, Costa Rica, Croatia, Ecuador, Egypt, El Salvador, Eritrea, Ethiopia, Honduras, India, Indonesia, Kenya, Madagascar, Malawi, Mali, Mauritania, Mauritius, Mexico, Morocco, Namibia, Nicaragua, Niger, Pakistan, Philippines, Senegal, South Africa, Swaziland, Tanzania, Turkey, Uganda, Zambia

Source: Staff calculations with various ICS data and Penn World Table data.

with taxes (bribes in taxes) and informality in general (losses due to criminal activity and security problems).

Our country measure of TFP^{IC} is highly correlated with the inverse of the ease of doing business.[32] Therefore, TFP^{IC} is useful to make cross-country comparisons and at the same time identify the main individual IC bottlenecks for improving country competitiveness.

The companies in Turkey are usually characterized by having higher entry and exit rates than similar emerging countries. Furthermore, those firms are in general of small size and only around 50 percent of them are able to survive after four years. Those negative business characteristics are consistent with having a bad IC, as we detected in our econometric application and finding dominant aggregate negative IC effects on TFP, see Figure 8.

---

[32] We consider the inverse of the ease of doing business since high values of the index are indicative of a bad business environment.

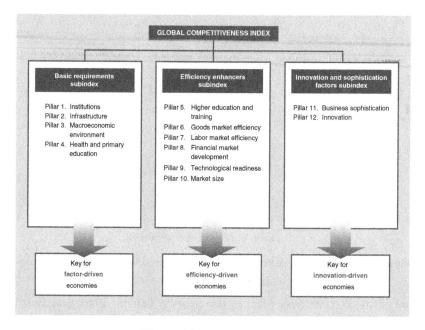

Figure 14 Pillars of the GCI

Source: World Economic Forum 2012.

The rest of this section illustrates the robustness capability of the TFP^{IC} measure to identify constraints, or bottlenecks, for growth in other countries by using a battery of other international economic performance indexes associated with the competitive environment. Figure 14 shows the twelve pillars selected in the GCI. In the first block, there is a list of four pillars related to basic requirements or factor-driven economies. Three of the four pillars are among those selected from the econometric analysis of the IC; institutions (in Turkey bad elements are selected, such as losses due to criminal activity, security problems, bribes paid for taxes, etc.), infrastructures (related to electricity problems) and macroeconomic environment (related to informal competition and trading across borders). The center block lists the main six efficiency enhancers and in Turkey four of the six became significant from the econometric analysis that was undertaken; higher education and training (training is one of IC variables selected), good and market efficiency (informal competition), financial market development (equity financing, sales after delivery) and technology readiness (Web page use). Clearly, from our analysis, Turkey is not in the last block of innovation-driven economies since neither of those two pillars (business sophistication and innovation) became significant.

Table 11 gives information on individual scores of the twelve pillars of the previously selected emerging countries. From the GCI score we can see that Turkey performs similarly to India, better than Brazil and worse than the rest. The key bad pillars for Turkey are indicated in bold numbers. Specific targets are innovations, labor market and product market and institutions.

Figures 15 and 16 show the cross-plots between the TFP^{IC} and the scores of GCI and with innovation block of the GCI, respectively. Both cross-country correlations are positive and very high, indicating that the TFP^{IC} is a good indicator of a country's competitiveness. Our aggregate TFP^{IC} measure associated with the country's IC is highly correlated with the GCI index, therefore the selected individual IC variables forming TFP^{IC} open the door for suggesting detailed policy analysis and reforms in those countries.

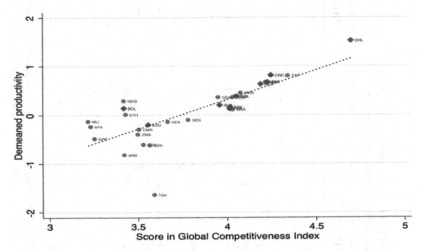

Figure 15 Cross-plot between the TFP^{IC} aggregate and the GCI score

Sample of 39 countries: Algeria, Bangladesh, Bolivia, Botswana, Brazil, Burkina Faso, Cameroon, Chile, Colombia, Costa Rica, Croatia, Ecuador, Egypt, El Salvador, Eritrea, Ethiopia, Honduras, India, Indonesia, Kenya, Madagascar, Malawi, Mali, Mauritania, Mauritius, Mexico, Morocco, Namibia, Nicaragua, Niger, Pakistan, Philippines, Senegal, South Africa, Swaziland, Tanzania, Turkey, Uganda, Zambia

Source: Staff calculations with various ICS data and Penn World Table data

Table 11 International scores in the global competitiveness reports

Series name	Brazil (2018)	Chile (2018)	China (2018)	India (2018)	Mexico (2018)	Turkey (2018)	Turkey (2008)
Global Competitiveness Index 4.0	59.5	70.3	72.6	62.0	64.6	61.6	42.5
1st pillar: Institutions	49.7	63.6	54.6	57.9	47.7	52.9	41.3
2nd pillar: Infrastructure	64.3	75.2	78.1	68.7	72.9	72.6	36.8
3rd pillar: ICT adoption	55.6	61.3	71.5	28.0	51.3	53.5	46.6
4th pillar: Macroeconomic stability	64.6	100.0	98.3	89.8	99.4	67.4	53.1
5th pillar: Health	79.6	93.4	87.0	59.0	84.6	86.2	40.5
6th pillar: Skills	56.0	69.6	64.1	54.5	57.9	60.5	45.4
7th pillar: Product market	48.9	68.2	57.4	50.9	57.5	55.2	36.0
8th catch: Labor market	51.0	63.2	59.3	58.3	54.4	51.2	44.0
9th pillar: Financial system	63.2	80.3	71.9	69.5	60.8	59.9	33.9
10th pillar: Market size	80.9	62.7	100.0	92.7	80.6	78.5	49.7
11th pillar: Business dynamism	52.4	64.3	64.6	61.2	65.5	57.2	44.5
12th pillar: Innovation capability	47.8	41.3	64.4	53.8	42.7	44.0	33.6

Source: World Economic Forum, 2020; Authors' calculations with data from IC surveys, Turkey 2008 ES and Turkey 2018 ES.

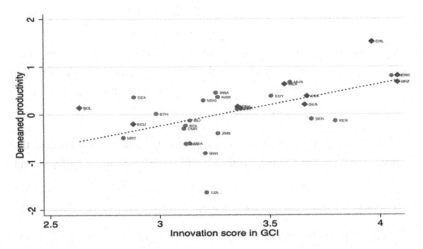

Figure 16 Cross-plot between TFP^{IC} aggregate and the score in the Innovation pillar of the GCI

Sample of 39 countries: Algeria, Bangladesh, Bolivia, Botswana, Brazil, Burkina Faso, Cameroon, Chile, Colombia, Costa Rica, Croatia, Ecuador, Egypt, El Salvador, Eritrea, Ethiopia, Honduras, India, Indonesia, Kenya, Madagascar, Malawi, Mali, Mauritania, Mauritius, Mexico, Morocco, Namibia, Nicaragua, Niger, Pakistan, Philippines, Senegal, South Africa, Swaziland, Tanzania, Turkey, Uganda, Zambia

Source: Staff calculations with various ICS data and Penn World Table data.

5 Evidence of the Robustness of TFP Measures and of the Empirical Results of the Effects of the IC

As additional insights into the robustness of the results found in Table 3, here we show the main moments of the eight TFP distributions and their corresponding kernel estimates of their density functions.

We start with a brief discussion on the relation of our measure TFP with standard measures of technical efficiency (TE). Following the literature on frontier production function, a TE measure was initially suggested by Debreu (1951) and Farrell (1957), where input prices are treated as exogenous (producers are price takers). Then following Green (2008), the Debreu-Farrell measure of technical efficiency is related with our measure of TFP coming from equation (1a), without taking logs. That is,

$$TE_{it} = \frac{Y_{it}}{F(L_{it}, M_{it}, K_{it}, \alpha)} = TFP_{it} \leq 1 \tag{43}$$

Where the function F(.) is a Cobb-Douglas production function. Therefore, $\log TFP_{it}$ (or TFP_{it}) from (44) should be negative, having a negative mean (negative constant term). However, when we estimate the constant term $(\hat{\alpha}_P)$ of (45) it is only negative in 2 of the eight TFP measures; see Figure 17a.

Consider the TFP measured with the *a non 0 mean* given by equation (45),

$$y_{it} = \hat{\alpha}_L l_{it} + \hat{\alpha}_M m_{it} + \hat{\alpha}_K k_{it} + \hat{tfp}_{it}. \tag{44}$$

However, the TFP measure *with a 0 mean* is $\hat{tfp}_{it}^d$ and it is obtained as the residuals of the estimated equation (45) where $\hat{\alpha}_p = E(\hat{tfp}_{it})$ and $\hat{tfp}_{it}^d = \hat{tfp}_{it} - E(\hat{tfp}_{it})$,

$$y_{it} = \hat{\alpha}_L l_{it} + \hat{\alpha}_M m_{it} + \hat{\alpha}_K k_{it} + \hat{\alpha}_P + \hat{tfp}_{it}^d. \tag{45}$$

The reason for including this second productivity measure from equation (45) is to consider only the idiosyncratic productivity shocks at the firm level, isolating constant technical efficiency, which is probably the main source of inconsistencies among TFP measures.[33]

Figures 17a and 17b show the estimated kernel densities for the eight TFP measures considered throughout this Element. In the upper panel (Figure 17a) the TFP measures include the constant technical efficiency. As can be seen, when this ET is included, the productivity measures have very different location (mean), which is also reflected in the heterogeneity of some of the correlations of Table 12.

However, when we only eliminate the constant technical efficiency term (see lower panel in Figure 17b) it is observed that the TFP measures are similar, once they have centered on a similar 0 mean and with a similar standard deviations. The bivariate correlations between the eight TFP measures of Figure 17b, without constant technical efficiency, are listed in Table 12 (lower panel) and in all the cases are now above 0.9. However, notice from the top panel of Table 12 that when they are not centered, the correlation with the Translog (unrestricted)[34] is close to 0. Figure 17c shows that to get robust TFP measures it is not enough to subtract the constant ET from the TFP in (25) to obtain the centered TFP.

In summary, after excluding the constant terms and the dummies for industries and regions from the eight TFP measures, we get our suggested measure

---

[33] We include in Figures 17b and 17c the productivity (TFP) measures without the constant term and without industry dummies, respectively, because the constant is likely to be estimated inconsistently.

[34] In other emerging countries these correlations among TFP measures could be negative but still the IC effects on those different TFP measures are robust.

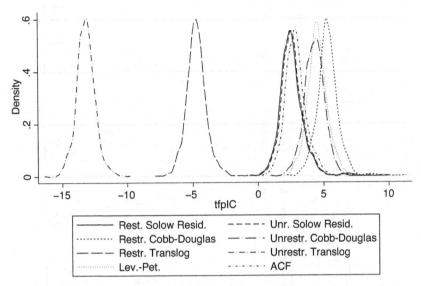

Figure 17a Estimated kernel densities of alternative TFP measures *with* constant technical efficiency terms included

Source: Authors' calculations with data from Turkey 2018 ES.

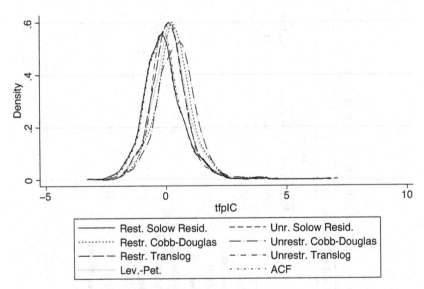

Figure 17b Estimated kernel densities of alternative TFP measures *without* the constant TE terms and <u>without</u> dummies for industries and regions (TFP^{IC})

Source: Authors' calculations with data from Turkey 2018 ES.

of TFP measure to be used for international robust TFP comparisons, (TFP^{IC}); that is, *the part of TFP that is only associated with the investment climate of each country.* The first two moments of the TFP^{IC} distributions (mean and

Table 12 Correlations between productivity measures, with and without constant technical efficiency terms, Turkey 2018 ES

With constant technical efficiency

		Two-step		Single-step				Two-step	
		Restricted Solow res.	Restricted Solow res.	Restricted CD	Unrestricted CD	Translog restricted	Translog unrestricted	LP	ACF
Two-step	Restricted Solow res.	1.000							
	Restricted Solow res.	0.997	1.000						
Single-step	Restricted CD	0.935	0.934	1.000					
	Unrestricted CD	0.522	0.501	0.598	1.000				
	Translog restricted	0.877	0.874	0.932	0.558	1.000			
	Translog unrestricted	0.046	0.096	0.072	−0.046	0.054	1.000		
Two-step	LP	0.966	0.964	0.990	0.581	0.925	0.074	1.000	
	ACF	0.997	0.994	0.946	0.535	0.887	0.048	0.971	1.000

Without constant technical efficiency

		Two-step		Single-step				Two-step	
		Restricted Solow res.	Restricted Solow res.	Restricted CD	Unrestricted CD	Translog restricted	Translog unrestricted	LP	ACF
Two-step	Restricted Solow res.	1.000							
	Restricted Solow res.	0.999	1.000						
Single-step	Restricted CD	0.942	0.943	1.000					
	Unrestricted CD	0.903	0.902	0.962	1.000				
	Translog restricted	0.882	0.881	0.927	0.917	1.000			
	Translog unrestricted	0.826	0.827	0.876	0.908	0.944	1.000		
Two-step	LP	0.968	0.967	0.992	0.955	0.924	0.870	1.000	
	ACF	0.997	0.996	0.951	0.913	0.890	0.836	0.972	1.000

Source: Authors' calculations with data from Turkey 2018 ES.

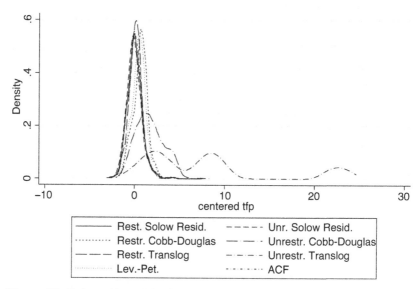

Figure 17c Estimated kernel densities of alternative TFP measures only *without* the TE constant term (centered-TFP)

Source: Authors' calculations with data from Turkey 2018 ES.

variance) and the shape of the whole density functions of TFP^{IC} are very similar in Figure 17b. Furthermore, in this case, we also get similar bivariate correlations among the eight TFP^{IC} measures; all correlations are close to 0.9 (bottom panel of Table 12). However, notice that this robustness property is lost if we only subtract the constant TE term; see Figure 17c. The main changes occur when we allow the input-output elasticities to vary by industry (unrestricted Cobb-Douglas and unrestricted Translog) since in those cases the location parameter (mean) of the centered TFP and also the shape of the whole distribution change a lot.

Finally, as evidence of additional robustness of how the IC affect TFP, we estimate a short panel of observations available for the Turkey 2012 ES and Turkey 2018 ES. That is, of the 1,112 companies in the 2018 survey, 439 companies were also in 2012. For the estimation we repeat the values of the 2018 IC variables in 2012 (IC as observable fixed-effects as suggested initially by Escribano and Guasch (2004, 2005). The idea is to check if the IC results on TFP change or not in maintaining the same IC in both years. The results in Table 13 are very robust to the inclusion of this second year IC information. All the elasticities and semi-elasticities of the IC variables on TFP maintain their sign obtained by using only data from Turkey 2018 ES.

Table 13 Estimates using panel data 2012–18 (two years), repeating 2018 data for the IC variables

	Two-step		Single-step				Two steps	
	Restricted Solow res.	Restricted Solow res.	Restricted CD	Unrestricted CD	Restricted Translog	Unrestricted Translog	LP	ACF
Electricity generator	−0.365 (0.236)	−0.356 (0.238)	−0.124 (0.224)	−0.0779 (0.209)	−0.0235 (0.202)	−0.0625 (0.211)	−0.573** (0.192)	−0.748*** (0.192)
Loses due to criminal activity	−0.178 (0.102)	−0.162 (0.104)	−0.167 (0.114)	−0.203 (0.116)	−0.145 (0.127)	−0.146 (0.133)	−0.468*** (0.0591)	−0.401*** (0.0624)
Security	−0.187 (0.294)	−0.178 (0.284)	−0.163 (0.286)	−0.0852 (0.268)	−0.220 (0.286)	−0.293 (0.301)	−0.222 (0.218)	−0.408 (0.211)
Tax inspections	−0.00782 (0.00929)	−0.00709 (0.00908)	−0.00896 (0.00702)	−0.0136 (0.00756)	−0.00892 (0.00778)	−0.0114 (0.00695)	−0.00946 (0.00943)	−0.0119 (0.00994)
Informal comp.	−0.120 (0.231)	−0.134 (0.229)	−0.169 (0.217)	−0.431 (0.234)	−0.171 (0.213)	−0.331 (0.207)	−0.322 (0.174)	−0.223 (0.181)
Bribes in taxes	−6.327*** (1.307)	−6.229*** (1.314)	−5.803*** (1.186)	−4.571*** (0.951)	−4.353*** (1.200)	−2.794* (1.167)	−2.740* (1.066)	−3.688*** (1.029)
Equity financing	0.837** (0.313)	0.796* (0.308)	0.761* (0.298)	0.687* (0.283)	0.553* (0.268)	0.425 (0.282)	0.472* (0.211)	0.536* (0.225)

Table 13 (cont.)

	Two-step		Single-step				Two steps	
	Restricted Solow res.	Restricted Solow res.	Restricted CD	Unrestricted CD	Restricted Translog	Unrestricted Translog	LP	ACF
Sales after delivery	0.373	0.354	0.361	0.301	0.364	0.451	0.365	0.329
	(0.322)	(0.320)	(0.311)	(0.303)	(0.304)	(0.287)	(0.249)	(0.255)
Web page use	0.000307	0.000308	0.00107	0.000704	0.000578	0.0000580	−0.00715***	−0.00917***
	(0.00365)	(0.00367)	(0.00387)	(0.00373)	(0.00360)	(0.00332)	(0.00187)	(0.00174)
Training	0.00114	0.00114	0.00161	0.00116	0.00164	0.00133	0.000970	0.000304
	(0.00114)	(0.00116)	(0.00113)	(0.00109)	(0.00113)	(0.00117)	(0.00104)	(0.000998)
Age	−0.125**	−0.123**	−0.0443	−0.0260	−0.0338	−0.0288	0.0427	−0.0227
	(0.0457)	(0.0457)	(0.0515)	(0.0447)	(0.0475)	(0.0434)	(0.0383)	(0.0397)
N	1551	1,551	1,551	1,551	1,551	1,551	1,112	1,112
R^2	0.110	0.109	0.729	0.742	0.746	0.787	0.157	0.134

Source: Authors' calculations with data from Turkey 2012 ES and Turkey 2018 ES.

6 International Countries' Investment Climate Assessments Based on Enterprise Business Surveys of Other Selected Emerging Countries and Regions

Basic references of the relevance of the IC analysis for international country reports are the annual World Bank reports of 2003, 2004a, 2004b, the more recent reports of 2010a, 2010b and 2011 and the survey of Dethier, Hirn and Straub (2008).

The ESs are intended to be representative of the whole private sector, covering information on a wide range of business-related areas such as access to finance, corruption, infrastructure, crime, competition, as well as economic performance measures (i.e., sales, employment, investment, exporting activity, innovation, etc.). Survey collection began in 2001. A common methodology for the data compilation wase developed in 2005 and it has been applied ever since: around 164,000 firms in 144 countries have been interviewed using this common methodology. The earlier ESs provided information on firms' production function variables (i.e., revenue, employment, capital and materials), for two or three years based on recall data, that is, firms' managers were asked to provide information on these variables for the year in which the survey was conducted plus one or two previous years. Currently, each ES only gives information on the production function variables for a single year. However, some firms are interviewed over several years, which allows constructing panel datasets of up to three years but with large gaps in between each time period of observations.[35]

6.1 Africa

Escribano, Guasch and Pena (2010), applied these type of microeconometric techniques to IC surveys, or ESs, of twenty-six African[36] countries carried out in different years from 2002 to 2006.

Disentangling the ways that infrastructure affects Africa's economic growth poses several difficulties because of the special characteristics of the African region. The comprehensive analysis found in Estache (2005) takes stock of the basic characteristics of infrastructure in sub-Saharan Africa and the effect of

---

[35] The Enterprise Surveys (ESs): www.enterprisesurveys.org/.

[36] These 26 countries show enormous heterogeneity due to (a) geographical factors, such as whether a nation is landlocked (Cape Verde, Madagascar, and Mauritius), tropical (with landmass for the most part covered by rainforests), or dominated by deserts (such as the North African countries Mauritania and Namibia); (b) social or political factors, such as civil wars, armed conflicts, early democracies, dictatorships, and colonial heritage; and (c) economic factors, which this paper discusses for all countries, from the most affluent (Mauritius) to the poorest (Eritrea). Among these 26 countries analyzed with this econometric methodology, the clearest case of emerging economy is South Africa.

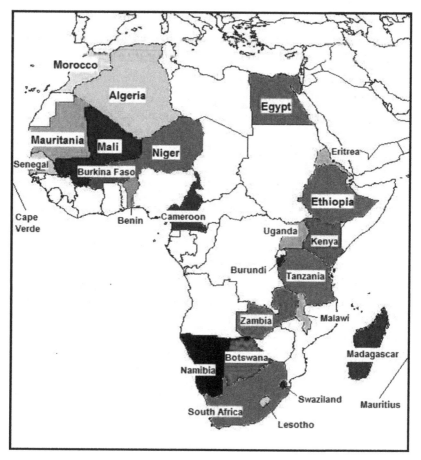

Figure 18 African countries considered in the econometric analysis

Source: Escribano, Guasch and Pena (2010).

1990 reforms, pointing out that the impact of infrastructure in Africa may be different than in other regions. As Brunel (2004) notes, the colonial period has had a lasting effect on the use of space in the region, resulting in a productive structure that consists, in most cases, of coastal cities connected inland by railways designed to carry raw materials to main ports. This and other factors that are progressively modifying the continent's productive structure – such as continuous urbanization, the movement of economic activity from the agricultural to manufacturing and service sectors, and the increasing openness of African economies – has caused both a quantitative and qualitative mismatch between the current supply of infrastructure and an ever-increasing demand. Factors such as inequality across income levels (affecting the affordability of infrastructure services), large and unoccupied areas, and regional variations in climate are increasingly becoming a concern for African policymakers managing infrastructure.

In addition to furthering the regional integration needed to support infrastructure investment, African governments made important contributions to infrastructure development in the decades following independence. The majority of African state monopolies were, however, characterized by inefficient bureaucracies. These became increasingly unable to satisfy customer demands, developing increasing deficits. By the beginning of the 1980s, most African countries embarked on infrastructure sector reforms, with the aim of increasing private sector participation in provision. Despite attempts to introduce more competition and attract private investors, Africa continues to trail the behind the rest of the world in both the quantity and quality of its infrastructure, with bottlenecks particularly in the management of current stock.

Olley and Pakes (1996) made country-specific evaluations of the impact of IC quality on aggregate TFP, average TFP, and allocative efficiency. For each country, they evaluated the IC impact based on ten different firm-level productivity measures. Economic impacts are robust for all different productivity measures used, once observable fixed effects (red tape, corruption and crime; finance; innovation and labor skills, etc.), obtained from the ICSs, are controlled for. They rank African countries according to several indices: per capita income, ease of doing business, firm perceptions of growth bottlenecks and the concept of IC related productivity obtained from firm-level data. Improvements in IC-related productivity will lead to higher per capita income levels.

They divided countries into two blocks: high-income growth and low-income growth. Infrastructure quality has a low impact on TFP in countries of the first block and a high (negative) impact in countries of the second block. Important conclusions are that, poor-quality electricity provision affects productivity of mainly poor countries, whereas problems dealing with customs while importing or exporting affect productivity of mainly faster-growing countries; losses from transport interruptions affect productivity of mainly slower-growing countries and water outages affect mainly slower-growing countries.

6.2 Latin America and Caribbean (LAC)

An overview of the IC in Latin America and Caribbean (LAC) is provided by Fajnzylber, Guasch and López (2009) and by recent World Bank IC reports. However, here we briefly present the main empirical results of Escribano and Guasch (2004, 2005), which are the two seminal works proposing the robust methodology described and developed in this Element, for alternative TFP measures.

We begin with a brief description of the main characteristics of their database, a short unbalanced panel of three countries: Guatemala, Honduras and Nicaragua. They have temporal observations (T = 2) for the years 2001 and 2002 (recall data) for all the variables of the production function (Y, L, M, K) except for the IC variables, for which there are observations only for the year 2002. This issue raises the first question: should we only use cross-sectional data (say only for 2002) or should we also use the data of the year 2001, even if we do not have information on the IC variables for that year? To address this issue, one can assume that, unless there is a structural break in the economy, the IC variables should not change that much from one year to the next. In fact, what can change from one year to the next is the reaction of the firm facing certain ICs, but that depends on the firm perceptions of the impact of IC variables and on the time required for the firm to implement those desired changes. In the empirical application, Escribano and Guasch maintained the IC coefficients constant and added some temporal dummies, thus affecting the constant term of the productivity equations in each year.

Since Escribano and Guasch were interested in having as many observations as possible, to benefit from the *law of large numbers*, they suggested to pool the data from the three countries and later analyze their differences and similarities. This is important because the observations are very unevenly distributed through time and across firms, precluding doing a separate country analysis of each industry. For example, for an industry analysis country by country, there is a textile sector in Honduras with only nine observations, while pooling the observations from the three countries results in at least thirty-eight observations in that sector, thus giving more reliable statistical results.

In the year 2001, after pooling the observations from the three countries, they had only 441 observations while for year 2002 they had 1,020 observations. Therefore, if they had measured productivity using rates of growth they would have at most 441 firms, which is a very small sample size to study differences by industry and by country. However, analysis in levels or logs would yield 1,461 observations in total which would provide more reliable statistical results.

Escribano and Guasch's estimates show consistent effects across different TFP measures. Overall, they account for over 30 percent of TFP. The two most impactful categories are red tape, corruption and crime, and infrastructure, accounting, respectively, for about 12 and 9 percent of TFP. As Perry et al. (2007) note, "The importance of reducing informality requires action to increase aggregate productivity in the economy. . . .. Although the study focuses on Latin America, its analysis, approach and conclusions are relevant for all developing countries."

6.3 India

An overview of the IC of India is given in Ferrari and Dhingra (2009). The main results obtained by Escribano and co-authors for the productivity manufacturing sector, are briefly summarized here, where the relative importance of IC variables in terms of contributions to average log-productivity at the aggregate level is separated by blocks. The infrastructure block represents 29.4 percent of the whole contribution of IC and C variables to average log-productivity (TFP); within these factors are the longest time spent dealing with customs to export, having to own a generator, the percentage of water supply from public source, having own transport and firms regularly using their Web page to communicate with their clients and suppliers. The largest contribution comes from the longest days to clear customs to export goods. Other control variables is the second block of variables in order of importance representing 27.1 percent of the whole contribution of IC variables to average log-productivity. The main key factors of this group of variables are: the age of the firm, the share of direct exports, the percentage of workforce unionized and the dummy variable identifying medium-sized firms. The block of red tape, corruption and crime's relative importance with respect to all IC variables in productivity equation is 18.8 percent. Within this group, firms' productivity is affected by informalities in the relations between firms and the government such as having the advantage of speeding up bureaucracy via informal payments or the possibility of maintaining a percentage of sales undeclared to tax authorities; on the other hand, if firms have security costs or illegal payments for protection, their productivity is negatively affected. The largest contribution comes from the variable measuring security problems.

The next IC block in order of importance is finance and corporate governance, with a relative impact on average log-productivity of 16.7 percent. Five variables within this group affect the TFP equation: belonging to a chamber of commerce, percentage of firm's capital owned by the largest shareholder, percentage of borrowing denominated in foreign currency, firm access to a loan line and if the firm has its annual statements externally audited, with the largest shareholder variable providing the largest contribution.

The last IC block in order of TFP importance is quality, innovation and labor skills for which the relative weight within all IC variables is 8 percent. The factors of this group affecting productivity are: if the firm has performed R&D activities, if the plant uses technology licensed from a foreign company, the percentage of workforce receiving internal training and the percentage of staff using computers at their job. The largest contributions to average log-productivity within this group come from unskilled workforce and dummy for R&D.

Similar productivity analysis was done by Escribano and co-authors using World Bank reports about India, based on the *retail sector* and the *software and information technology enable services* (ITES), two very important economic sectors in India. For a selection of the main econometric results, see Ferrari and Dhingra (2009). However, it is noteworthy that informality and missing observations were two key aspects of the retail sector in India. In fact, without imputation of missing values (complete case), the econometric analysis of the productivity of the retail sector could not have been done due to a serious problem of omitted variables in certain key variables having a high percentage of missing observations.

Further evidence on other Asian countries can be found in Escribano et al. (2009) where they show empirical evidence on the IC effects on several economic performance measures, including TFP, probability of exporting and probability of attraction of foreign direct investment (FDI), etc., of Indonesia, Malaysia, Philippines and Thailand.

7 Conclusions and Further Extensions

The analysis of the institutional, social, political and economic arrangements that a society employs in the production of goods and services – the investment or business enterprise climate for us – has become a key instrument for developing countries aiming to identify and improve the main economic obstacles to business competitiveness and growth.

The aim of the econometric approach discussed in this Element, was to identify and assess the importance of providing robust empirical regularities of the IC factors associated with the productivity of firms in emerging countries. We found IC elasticities and semi-elasticities on TFP that are robust to alternative productivity environments (assumptions). Obviously, the results are not numerically identical among the different TFP specifications, but the observed variation in the parameter estimates is reasonable and gives credibility to the signs and magnitudes for policy analysis.

The econometric evaluation is not a simple task due to the many methodological difficulties we have encountered, among them: regressor endogeneity, alternative productivity measures (TFPs), model selection strategies, multicollinearity and low quality of the ES database of emerging countries (missing observations, outliers, etc.). Despite all these difficulties, we believe that the estimated empirical regularities given for the case of Turkey, as an example, are useful.

If the TFP of Turkey's manufacturing sector were equal to 100, the IC associated with TFP would represent about 35.8 percent. This is what we call TFP^{IC}.

In Turkey, this overall contribution of TFP^{IC} is negative, which means that, in general, the IC tends to pose difficulties (constraints) to the competitiveness of firms and therefore limits the efficiency of the manufacturing sector in Turkey. Of this negative contribution, a large proportion, say 85 percent, is driven by the effect of average TFP on the average firm. Also, the average negative TFP effect is cushioned by the allocative efficiency effect. This allocative effect only accounts for 15 percent of the IC effect on the aggregate TFP. A greater importance of this distributional effect across firms could have further reduced the negative IC effect of the average TFP.

Most of the negative IC effects, in Turkey, are associated with the block of red tape, corruption and crime and, therefore in general, with the low quality of the institutions – such as informality. Obviously, there are also IC effects that are positively associated with TFP, such as use of the company Web page and the available training programs for company workers. However, the importance of these positive IC effects of TFP is lower than for the negative effects. Clearly, one way to improve the aggregate IC (TFP^{IC}) for doing business, while boosting the competitiveness of Turkish enterprises, is to implement policies aimed at reducing the impact of the negative aspects of the IC, while enhancing the positive aspects. We have seen that these goals can be achieved through increases in the average TFP effect, the allocative efficiency effect or through a combination of both.

The introduction of this econometric methodology on productivity for emerging countries was one of the main objectives of this Element. Therefore, in Appendix B we provide the do-file of STATA that would allow the reader to calculate all the results presented in this Element. A second objective of this Element was to obtain strong partial IC effects on alternative TFP measures. We have demonstrated that our estimates produced robust empirical TFP impacts across: (1) different *functional forms* of production functions, (2) different *measures of productivity,* and (3) *different levels of aggregation of input-output* elasticities (at the industry and country levels). We were able to obtain all the expected signs in all the IC coefficients.

Due to the empirical robustness of the IC effects on TFP obtained with this methodology, for a detailed individual IC variable evaluation we concentrate only on the set of empirical results obtained from our baseline model: for instance, the restricted Solow residuals (TFP) of the production function.[37]

---

[37] The question of how to make country comparisons of TFP, avoiding the problem of comparing apples and oranges, is addressed in this Element by using the concept of TFP^{IC} that measures the IC impacts on TFP of each country. This analysis could also be done at the aggregate level, industry by industry, region by region or by comparing particular blocks of IC variables; say infrastructures, as we did with 26 countries in Africa, see Escribano, Guasch and Pena (2010).

We have also shown that the alternative estimated aggregate TFP measures based on TFP^{IC} have densities functions that are very similar across eight TFP measures; they are robust. However, this is not the case of the other estimated TFP measures – estimated values of TFP nor the estimated centered TFP. Therefore, for cross-country TFP comparisons we suggest using the aggregate measure of TFP associated with the IC; TFPIC. We do this international analysis for selected emerging economies such as Brazil, Chile, India and Mexico. Finally, we do a larger international analysis of thirty-nine countries, by comparing their corresponding aggregate values of TFP^{IC} with the corresponding values of the GDP per capita, the scores obtained in the Doing Business reports of the World Bank and the performing scores obtained in the GCI of the World Economic Forum. The correlation with TFP^{IC} was very high in all those cases. Therefore, we expect that the significant individual IC variables obtained from the econometric analysis of each of the thirty-nine countries could open the door for suggesting plausible economic and regulatory reforms in each country in order to improve the business enterprise environment.

This Element has mainly concentrated on the methodology for the IC analysis on TFP, based on firm level data obtained from ESs. However, these ESs also contain other interesting information on relevant economic variables measuring *business performance*, such as exports, foreign direct investment (FDI), employment, wages, etc. This robustness approach could be extended to the TFP effects on those economic performance measures. For further information, interested readers should check the application given in Escribano et al. (2009) applied to several South East Asian countries.

Appendix A

Productivity in Levels (or Logs) versus Productivity in Differences (or Rates of Growth)

Productivity, or multifactor productivity (MFP), refers to the effects of any economic variable different from the inputs – labor (L), intermediate materials (M) and capital services (K) – affecting the production (sales) process. To be more specific, consider that the general production function

$$Q_{it} = F(L_{it}, M_{it}, K_{it}, MFP_{it}) \tag{A.1}$$

of the firm (i) in period (t), where the variable MFP_{it} is an aggregate productivity index which reflects technological changes, product and process innovations, and in general the business conditions or IC of each firm that affects the production of Y_{it}.

In this general specification, any improvement in MFP_{it}, perhaps due to improvements in IC conditions, represents either movements along the production function or a shift of the production function.

Total differentiation of equation (A.1) produces equation (A.2),

$$d\log Y_{it} = \frac{\partial \log F_{it}}{\partial L_{it}} dL_{it} + \frac{\partial \log F_{it}}{\partial M_{it}} dM_{it} + \frac{\partial \log F_{it}}{\partial K_{it}} dK_{it} + \frac{\partial \log F_{it}}{\partial MFP_{it}} dMFP_{it}. \tag{A.2}$$

Let the last term of equation (A.2), which is the elasticity ($\alpha_{MFP,it}$) weighted rate of growth of MFP_{it}, be written as,

$$\frac{\partial \log F_{it}}{\partial MFP_{it}} dMFP_{it} = \frac{\partial F_{it}}{\partial MFP_{it}} \frac{MFP_{it}}{F_{it}} \frac{dMFP_{it}}{MFP_{it}} = \alpha_{P,it} d\log MFP_{it}. \tag{A.3}$$

Doing similar transformations for each of the inputs (L, M and K) of equation (A.2) we get the general expression of the rate of growth of the firm's production in terms of the rates of growth of the inputs and the MFP term, weighted by the corresponding input-output elasticities:

$$d\log Y_{it} = \alpha_{L,it} d\log L_{it} + \alpha_{M,it} d\log M_{it} + \alpha_{K,it} d\log K_{it} + \alpha_{MFP,it} d\log MFP_{it}. \tag{A.4}$$

The MFP is unobserved and it can be obtained as the residual of equation (A.4),

$$\alpha_{it}d\log MFP_{it} = \log Y_{it} - \alpha_{L,it}d\log L_{it} - \alpha_{M,it}dM_{it} - \alpha_{K,it}dK_{itt}. \qquad (A.5)$$

However, when the separability conditions (Hicks-neutral technical change, etc.) are satisfied (see Jorgenson, Gollop and Fraumeni, 1987), $\alpha_{it} = 1$ and the "residual" (A.5) is the rate of growth of total factor productivity (dlogTFP). Under those conditions the production function (A.1) becomes,

$$Y_{it} = F(L_{it}, M_{it}, K_{it},) TFP_{it} \qquad (A.6)$$

and equation (A.5) becomes,

$$d\log TFP_{it} = \log Y_{it} - \alpha_{L,it}d\log L_{it} - \alpha_{M,it}d\log M_{it} - \alpha_{K,it}d\log K_{it} \qquad (A.7)$$

which is the basic equation of the *growth accounting technique*. Growth accounting techniques have been widely use, using the databases of the EU KLEMS (2017, 2018), to explain why Europe has experienced a slowed-down growth since 1990 while US productivity growth has sped up; refer to Mas and Robeldo (2010), Timmer et al. (2010), Aza (2017) and Perez et al. (2017). For the development of growth accounting techniques see Jorgenson and Griliches (1967) and Jorgenson et al. (1987).

In order to estimate productivity growth based on equation (A.7) we have to make two important decisions:

First. We have to approximate the continuous transformation of the variables, say $d\log(Y_{it})$, by a discrete approximation based on first differences, say $\Delta\log(Y_{it}) = \log(Y_{it})-\log(Y_{i,t-1})$. This last approximation requires transforming equation (A.7) using the Tornqvist (1936) index to obtain,

$$\Delta\log TFP_{it} = \Delta\log Y_{it} - \bar{a}_{L,it}\Delta\log L_{it} - \bar{a}_{M,it}\Delta\log M_{it} - \bar{a}_{K,it}\Delta\log K_{it} \qquad (A.8)$$

where $\bar{a}_{J,it} = \frac{1}{2}(a_{J,it} + a_{J,it-1})$ is average input-output elasticity of input J of firm i of the last two years (t and t-1) where J = L, M and K.

Second. Since heterogeneity at the firm level and time-varying input-output elasticities $\alpha_{J,it}$ are unknown, they can be measured by nonparametric procedures, index number techniques (see Solow, 1957; Diewert and Nakamura, 2003) or estimated by regression techniques, assuming in the last case that the input-output elasticity parameters are constant; $\alpha_{J,it} = \alpha_J$ for J = L, M and K, or allowing them to vary by industry. In the empirical application of this Element to Turkey, we have considered two possibilities; constant input-output elasticities by industry (unrestricted case) and constant elasticity parameters at the aggregate level (restricted case).

The following assumptions are needed to estimate the input-output elasticities using growth accounting techniques:

Assumption A.1: The technology of F(L,M,K) has constant returns to scale (CRS).

Assumption A.2: The product markets are competitive.

Assumption A.3: The input markets are competitive.

The CRS condition implies that $\alpha_{L,it} + \alpha_{M,it} + \alpha_{K,it} = 1$ and therefore equation (A.8) becomes,

$$\Delta logTFP_{it} = \Delta logY_{it} - \overline{\alpha}_{L,it}\Delta logL_{it} - \overline{\alpha}_{M,it}\Delta logM_{it}$$
$$- (1 - \overline{\alpha}_{L,it} - \overline{\alpha}_{M,it})\Delta logK_{it}. \qquad (A.9)$$

If assumptions A.1, A.2 and A.3 are satisfied, as was assumed by Solow (1957), we can calculate the Solow residuals using the *income-share* of each input to estimate the input-output elasticities for each firm i in every year t. A less restrictive growth accounting approach was suggested by Hall (1990) that only requires assumption A.1 and A.2 and measures the time-varying input-output elasticities by the corresponding *cost-share* of each input (Griliches, 1996).

This last approach is the growth accounting technique implemented in the productivity methodology used in this Element, but applied to the variables without differencing as in equation (A.10), where the variables are in levels (or in logs) to maintain the observable fixed effects related to the IC,

$$logTFP_{it} = logY_{it} - \alpha_0 - \overline{\alpha}_{L,it}logL_{it} - \overline{\alpha}_{M,it}logM_{it}$$
$$- (1 - \overline{\alpha}_{L,it} - \overline{\alpha}_{M,it})logK_{it}. \qquad (A.10)$$

In summary, the main advantage of using equation (A.10) to estimate TFP, (or logTFP), such as the Solow residuals is that we can allow input-output elasticities to vary by firm and by year, while having inputs that are not exogenous (endogenous), at the cost of assuming constant returns to scale and competitive inputs markets. The alternative approaches discussed here are based on different regression procedures that assume that input-output elasticities are constant but without having, necessarily, competitive inputs markets or constant returns to scale as will be discussed, but one would need to address the issue of having endogenous input variables (L, M and K), Haltiwanger (2002).

It will become clear why the particular characteristics of the World Bank ICs, or ESs, favor the productivity analysis done in levels.

Consider the production function (A.11a) together with the equation (A.11b) that makes clear that the total factor productivity depends on firm-level characteristics related to the business enterprise environment, investment climate (IC_{it}) and other firm-level control variables (C_{it}),

$$Y_{it} = F\left(L_{it}, \ M_{it}, \ K_{it}, \ \alpha_{J,it}\right) TFP_{it} \tag{A.11a}$$

$$TFP_{it} = G(IC_{it}, C_{it}, \alpha_{IC,it}) \ \exp(u_{it}) \tag{A.11b}$$

where u_{it} is a random error term with properties that will be specified later on. The individual firms are indicated by the sub-index i = 1, 2, ..., N, where N is the total number of firms in the sample and by the subindex time t = 1, 2, ..., T, where T is the total number of years in the sample. In the IC surveys, N is large and T is small (T = 1, 2, 3).

When any of the input variables (L, M and K) is influenced by common causes affecting TFP, like IC variables or other firm characteristic variables (C), we have a simultaneous equation problem; see Marschak and Andews, (1944), and Griliches and Mairesse, (1997). In general, we should expect TFP to be correlated with the inputs L, M and K, and therefore the inputs must be treated as endogenous regressors when estimating production functions. Blundell and Bond (2000) discuss System-GMM, a solution to this endogenous regressors problem based on a generalized method of moments (GMM) approach, applied to persistent panel data. Olley and Pakes (1996), Levinsohn and Petrin (2003) and Ackerberg, Caves and Frazer (2015) suggested alternative structural approaches to estimate production functions, as was discussed in Section 2.2 of this Element.

As we demonstrated before, here we have total differentiation of equations (A.11a) and (A.11b),

$$d\mathrm{log}Y_{it} = \alpha_{L,it}d\mathrm{log}L_{it} + \alpha_{M,it}d\mathrm{log}M_{it} + \alpha_{K,it}d\mathrm{log}K_{it} + d\mathrm{log}TFP_{it} \tag{A.12a}$$

$$d\mathrm{log}TFP_{it} = \alpha'_{IC,it}d\mathrm{log}IC_{it} + \alpha'_{IC,it}d\mathrm{log}C_{it} + du_{it}. \tag{A.12b}$$

If the inputs (L, M and K) are also affected by the IC and by some of the other firm level control variables (C) then the inputs in equation (A.12a) are endogenous and correlated with TFP.

One way to reduce the degree of endogeneity of the inputs is by substituting equation (A.12b) into equation (A.12a) to get an *extended production function in rates of growth*, as in Escribano and Stucchi (2013),

$$d\log Y_{it} = a_{L,it}d\log L_{it} + a_{M,it}d\log M_{it} + a_{K,it}d\log K_{it} + a'_{IC,it}d\log IC_{it}$$
$$+ a'_{C,it}d\log C_{it} + du_{it} \tag{A.13}$$

Applying the approximation to the continuous transformation of the variables, say $d\log(Y_{it})$, by a discrete approximation based on first differences, say $\Delta\log(Y_{it}) = \log(Y_{it}) - \log(Y_{i,t-1})$ we get the extended growth accounting equation,

$$\Delta\log Y_{it} = \bar{a}_{L,it}\Delta\log L_{it} + \bar{a}_{M,it}\Delta\log M_{it} + \bar{a}_{K,it}\Delta\log K_{it} + \bar{a}'_{IC,it}\Delta\log IC_{it}$$
$$+ \bar{a}'_{C,it}\Delta\log C_{it} + \Delta w_{it} \tag{A.14}$$

Equation (A.14) is the *extended growth accounting equation* that is usually estimated by using input-output tables to calculate the cost-shares or revenue-shares of each explanatory variable. See, for example, Timmer et al. (2010), Mas and Robledo (2010), Aza (2017), Pérez and Benages (2017), EU KLEMS (2017, 2018) and Aza and Escribano (2019a, 2019b) for European applications and Jorgenson (2001) and Jorgenson, Ho and Stiroh (2005) for United States applications. However, there are no input-output databases related to the IC of emerging or developing countries generally available and, therefore, we could not use this approach for the ESs databases of the World Bank.

From this discussion, two general regression approaches to measure the IC impact on total factor productivity (TFP) are available:

(a) A regression equation based on the rates of growth of variables,

$$\Delta\log Y_{it} = a_L\Delta\log L_{it} + a_M\Delta\log M_{it} + a_K\Delta\log K_{it} + \bar{a}'_{IC}\Delta\log IC_{it}$$
$$+ \bar{a}'_C\Delta\log C_{it} + \zeta_{itt} \tag{A.15}$$

(b) A regression equation based on variables in levels (or logs),

$$\log Y_{it} = a_L\log L_{it} + a_M\log M_{it} + a_K\log K_{it} + \bar{a}'_{IC}\log IC_{it}$$
$$+ \bar{a}'_C\log C_{it} + a_0 + \varepsilon_{it} \tag{A.16}$$

Which of the two approaches, (a) or (b), is more convenient to evaluate the impact of IC variables on TFP based on ES databases of emerging and developing countries?

At first sight, the procedure based on productivity growth seems to be more general and more convenient because it does not require us to specify a particular functional form of the production function F(L,M,K). However, it has serious drawbacks arising from the quality of the data (measurement errors and missing firm observations from one year to the next). The common drawbacks of estimating equation in rates of growth are:

(i) Measurement errors are enhanced by taking first differences,

(ii) When the inputs are not strictly exogenous (or "exogenous") the use of standard simultaneous equations implies problems and least squares estimators are inconsistent and biased. The most common solution requires the use of GMM estimators or instrumental variable (IV) estimators (refer to Wooldridge, 2002). However, equations with variables in differences suffer from the weak instruments problem that produces very poor parameter estimates (Chamberlain, 1982; Griliches and Mairesse, 1997). Blundell and Bond (2000) proposed an alternative GMM estimator for variables that have a slow speed of mean reversion (persistent).

(iii) We usually only have information on IC variables for a single year and we could treat them as fixed effects. However, if we compute TFP in rates of growth, we lose all unobservable fixed effects but we also lose all the information on the IC variables, the treatment of which is one of the main aims of the econometric analysis.

Appendix B

Stata Do-File that Replicates the Results

```
cd "/Users/jorgepena/Desktop/CAMBRIDGE/Turkey-2019-full data.dta/"
*
set more off
use Turkey_cs_1.dta, replace
*
gen M=(exp(m)-1)
gen rK=.15*(exp(k)-1)
g LC=exp(lc)-1
gen TC=LC+M+rK
gen sl=LC/TC
gen sm=M/TC
gen sk=1-sl-sm
*
bysort ind: egen usl=mean(sl)
bysort ind: egen usm=mean(sm)
bysort ind: egen usk=mean(sk)
*
egen rsl=mean(sl)
egen rsm=mean(sm)
egen rsk=mean(sk)
*
gen rsr=y-rsl*n-rsm*m-rsk*k
gen usr=y-usl*n-usm*m-usk*k
label var rsr "Unrestricted by Industry Solow residual"
label var usr "Restricted Solow residual"
*
gen ll2=n^2
gen lm2=m^2
gen lk2=k^2
gen lllm=n*m
gen lllk=n*k
gen lmlk=m*k
xi i.ind i.ind|n i.ind|m i.ind|k i.ind|ll2 i.ind|lm2 i.ind|lk2
i.ind|lllm ///
i.ind|lllk i.ind|lmlk
*
loc X v_powlos av_elecgen ///
         v_crimeloss av_segur v_taxinsp av_infcomp av_infpaytax ///
         v_fxa_equy v_sales_adl ///
         av_internet av_training
loc W v_age
loc D reg_* ind_*
*
```

```
corr y n m k av_elecgen ///
        v_crimeloss av_segur v_taxinsp av_infcomp av_infpaytax ///
        v_fxa_equy v_sales_adl ///
        av_internet av_training
*
egen clustervar=group(region ind)
*
qui reg rsr `X' `W' `D', r cl(clustervar)
estimates store Two_Steps_Rst
predict u, resid
foreach x of varlist `X' `W' {
     g cnt_`x'=_b[`x']*`x'
}
egen cnt_tot=rsum(cnt_*)
g tfpr1=cnt_tot+u
drop u cnt_*
*
*
qui reg usr `X' `W' `D', r cl(clustervar)
estimates store Two_Steps_Unr
predict u, resid
foreach x of varlist `X' `W' {
     g cnt_`x'=_b[`x']*`x'
}
egen cnt_tot=rsum(cnt_*)
g tfpr2=cnt_tot+u
drop u cnt_*
*
*
qui reg y n m k `X' `W' `D', r cl(clustervar)
g bn1=_b[n]
g bm1=_b[m]
g bk1=_b[k]
estimates store One_Step_CD_Rst
predict u, resid
foreach x of varlist `X' `W' {
     g cnt_`x'=_b[`x']*`x'
}
egen cnt_tot=rsum(cnt_*)
g tfpr3=cnt_tot+u
drop u cnt_*
*
*
qui reg y n m k _IindXn_* _IindXm_* _IindXk_* `X' `W' `D', r cl(clustervar)
g bn2=_b[n] if ind==1
g bm2=_b[m] if ind==1
g bk2=_b[k] if ind==1
```

```
*
forvalues s=2(1)6 {
      replace bn2 = _b[n] + _b[_IindXn_`s'] if ind==`s'
      replace bm2 = _b[m] + _b[_IindXm_`s'] if ind==`s'
      replace bk2 = _b[k] + _b[_IindXk_`s'] if ind==`s'
}
*
estimates store One_Step_CD_Unr
predict u, resid
foreach x of varlist `X' `W' {
      g cnt_`x' = _b[`x']*`x'
}
egen cnt_tot=rsum(cnt_*)
g tfpr4=cnt_tot+u
drop u cnt_*
*
*
qui reg y n m k ll2 lm2 lk2 lllm lmlk lllk `X' `W' `D', r cl(clustervar)
g bn3 = _b[n] + 2*_b[ll2]*n + _b[lllk]*k + _b[lllm]*m
g bm3 = _b[m] + 2*_b[lm2]*m + _b[lmlk]*k + _b[lllm]*n
g bk3 = _b[k] + 2*_b[lk2]*k + _b[lmlk]*m + _b[lllk]*n
*
estimates store One_Step_TR_Rst
predict u, resid
foreach x of varlist `X' `W' {
      g cnt_`x' = _b[`x']*`x'
}
egen cnt_tot=rsum(cnt_*)
g tfpr5=cnt_tot+u
drop u cnt_*
*
*
qui reg y n m k ll2 lm2 lk2 lllm lmlk lllk _IindXn_* _IindXm_* _IindXk_* _IindXll2_*
_IindXlm2_* ///
_IindXlk2_* _IindXlllm_* _IindXlllk_* _IindXlmlk_* `X' `W' `D', r cl(clustervar)
g bn4 = _b[n] + 2*_b[ll2]*n + _b[lllk]*k + _b[lllm]*m if ind==1
g bm4 = _b[m] + 2*_b[lm2]*m + _b[lmlk]*k + _b[lllm]*n if ind==1
g bk4 = _b[k] + 2*_b[lk2]*k + _b[lmlk]*m + _b[lllk]*n if ind==1
*
forvalues s=2(1)6 {
      replace bn4 = _b[n] + 2*_b[ll2]*n + _b[lllk]*k + _b[lllm]*m + _b[_IindXn_`s'] +
2*_b[_IindXll2_`s']*n + _b[_IindXlllk_`s']*k + _b[_IindXlllm_`s']*m if ind==`s'
      replace bm4 = _b[m] + 2*_b[lm2]*m + _b[lmlk]*k + _b[lllm]*n + _b[_IindXm_`s'] +
2*_b[_IindXlm2_`s']*m + _b[_IindXlmlk_`s']*k + _b[_IindXlllm_`s']*n if ind==`s'
      replace bk4 = _b[k] + 2*_b[lk2]*k + _b[lmlk]*m + _b[lllk]*n + _b[_IindXk_`s'] +
2*_b[_IindXlk2_`s']*k + _b[_IindXlmlk_`s']*m + _b[_IindXlllk_`s']*n if ind==`s'
}
```

```
estimates store One_Step_TR_Unr
predict u, resid
foreach x of varlist `X' `W' {
      g cnt_`x' = _b[`x'] * `x'
}
egen cnt_tot=rsum(cnt_*)
g tfpr6=cnt_tot+u
drop u cnt_*
*
*
g tfpr_lp=y-0.206*n-0.145*k-0.476*m
g bn5 = 0.206
g bm5 = 0.476
g bk5 = 0.145
g tfpr_acf=y-0.299*n-0.122*k-0.550*m
g bn6 = 0.299
g bm6 = 0.550
g bk6 = 0.122
*
*
preserve
collapse sl sm sk bn1 bm1 bk1 bn3 bm3 bk3 bn5 bm5 bk5 bn6 bm6 bk6
restore
preserve
collapse usl usm usk bn2 bm2 bk2 bn4 bm4 bk4, by(ind)
restore
*
qui reg tfpr_lp `X' `W' `D', r cl(clustervar)
estimates store LP
predict u, resid
foreach x of varlist `X' `W' {
      g cnt_`x' = _b[`x'] * `x'
}
egen cnt_tot=rsum(cnt_*)
g tfpr7=cnt_tot+u
drop u cnt_*
*
*
qui reg tfpr_acf `X' `W' `D', r cl(clustervar)
estimates store ACF
predict u, resid
foreach x of varlist `X' `W' {
      g cnt_`x' = _b[`x'] * `x'
}
egen cnt_tot=rsum(cnt_*)
g tfpr8=cnt_tot+u
```

```
drop u cnt_*
*
corr tfpr1 tfpr2 tfpr3 tfpr4 tfpr5 tfpr6 tfpr7 tfpr8
tabstat tfpr1 tfpr2 tfpr3 tfpr4 tfpr5 tfpr6 tfpr7 tfpr8, c(s) s(mean)
corr tfpr1 tfpr2 tfpr3 tfpr4 tfpr5 tfpr6 tfpr7 tfpr8
tabstat tfpr1 tfpr2 tfpr3 tfpr4 tfpr5 tfpr6 tfpr7 tfpr8, c(s) s(sd)
corr tfpr1 tfpr2 tfpr3 tfpr4 tfpr5 tfpr6 tfpr7 tfpr8
tabstat tfpr1 tfpr2 tfpr3 tfpr4 tfpr5 tfpr6 tfpr7 tfpr8, c(s) s(min)
corr tfpr1 tfpr2 tfpr3 tfpr4 tfpr5 tfpr6 tfpr7 tfpr8
tabstat tfpr1 tfpr2 tfpr3 tfpr4 tfpr5 tfpr6 tfpr7 tfpr8, c(s) s(max)
*
*
esttab Two_Steps_Rst Two_Steps_Unr One_Step_CD_Rst One_Step_CD_Unr///
One_Step_TR_Rst One_Step_TR_Unr LP ACF using example2.csv, keep(`X' `W') r2 replace
*
twoway (kdensity tfpr1) (kdensity tfpr2) (kdensity tfpr3) (kdensity tfpr4) (kdensity
tfpr5) ///
     (kdensity tfpr6) (kdensity tfpr7) (kdensity tfpr8), xtitle("tfpIC") ///
     ytitle(Density) legend(order(1 "Rest. Solow Resid." 2 "Unr. Solow Resid." ///
     3 "Restr. Cobb-Douglas" 4 "Unrestr. Cobb-Douglas" 5 "Restr. Translog" ///
     6 "Unrestr. Translog" 7 "Lev.-Pet." 8 "ACF")) scheme(s2mono) ///
     graphregion(fcolor(white) lcolor(white) ifcolor(white) ilcolor(white))
          gr display, xsiz(1.5) ysiz(1)
          gr export g.png, replace
          png2rtf using Figures.doc, g(g.png) replace
*
*STANDARIZED COEFFICIENTS
*
preserve
     /*
     foreach x in `X' `W' {
     qui su `x'
     replace `x' = (`x' - r(mean))/r(sd)
     }
     */
     reg rsr `X' `W' `D', r cl(clustervar)
     *
     loc Betas
     foreach x in av_elecgen ///
               v_crimeloss av_segur v_taxinsp av_infcomp av_infpaytax ///
               v_fxa_equy v_sales_adl ///
               av_internet av_training v_age {
               replace `x' = _b[`x']
               loc Betas `Betas' `x'
     }
     collapse `Betas'
```

```
    mkmat `Betas', mat(B)
    mat B=B'
    clear
    svmat B
    g cat=_n
    label def cat 1 "Elec. generator" ///
    3 "Security" ///
    4 "Tax inspections" ///
    5 "Informal comp." ///
    6 "Bribes in taxes" ///
    7 "Equity financing" ///
    8 "Sales after delivery" ///
    9 "Web page use" ///
    10 "Training" ///
    11 "Age"
    label value cat cat
    graph bar (mean) B, over(cat, label(angle(vertical) labsize(small))) ///
        bar(1, fcolor(blue)) bar(2, fcolor(ltblue)) ///
        bar(3, fcolor(ltbluishgray)) blabel(bar, orientation(vertical) format
(%9.2f)) ///
        ytitle(Value) ///
        graphregion(fcolor(white) lcolor(white) ifcolor(white) ilcolor(white))
        gr display, xsiz(1.5) ysiz(1)
        gr export g.png, replace
        png2rtf using Figures.doc, g(g.png) a
restore
*
*AVERAGE CONTRIBUTIONS
*
preserve
    reg rsr `X' `W' `D', r cl(clustervar)
    *
    loc Conts
    qui su rsr
    loc mrsr = r(mean)
    foreach x in av_elecgen ///
            v_crimeloss av_segur v_taxinsp av_infcomp av_infpaytax ///
            v_fxa_equy v_sales_adl ///
            av_internet av_training v_age {
            qui su `x'
            replace `x' = 100*((r(mean)*_b[`x'])/`mrsr')
            loc Conts `Conts' `x'
    }
    collapse `Conts'
    mkmat `Conts', mat(B)
    mat B=B'
    clear
```

```
svmat B
g cat=_n
label def cat 1 "Elec. generator" ///
2 "Crime loss." ///
3 "Security" ///
4 "Tax inspections" ///
5 "Informal comp." ///
6 "Bribes in taxes" ///
7 "Equity financing" ///
8 "Sales after delivery" ///
9 "Web page use" ///
10 "Training" ///
11 "Age"
label value cat cat
graph bar (mean) B, over(cat, label(angle(vertical) labsize(small))) ///
    bar(1, fcolor(blue)) bar(2, fcolor(ltblue)) ///
    bar(3, fcolor(ltbluishgray)) blabel(bar, orientation(vertical) format
(%9.2f)) ///
    ytitle(% Contribution) legend(order(1 "% Contribution to aggregate TFP
(ln)" ///
    2 "% Contribution to average TFP (ln)") rows(2)) ///
    graphregion(fcolor(white) lcolor(white) ifcolor(white) ilcolor(white))
    gr display, xsiz(1.5) ysiz(1)
    gr export g.png, replace
    png2rtf using Figures.doc, g(g.png) a
restore
*
*
*
loc X v_powlos av_elecgen ///
    v_crimeloss av_segur v_taxinsp av_infcomp av_infpaytax ///
    v_fxa_equy v_sales_adl ///
    av_internet av_training
loc W v_age
loc D reg_* ind_*
qui reg rsr `X' `W' `D', r cl(clustervar)
loc X av_elecgen ///
    v_crimeloss av_segur v_taxinsp av_infcomp av_infpaytax ///
    v_fxa_equy v_sales_adl ///
    av_internet av_training
foreach x of varlist `X' {
    g cn_`x' = `x'*abs(_b[`x'])
}
egen IC=rsum(cn_*)
*
*
*1. OP. Dec.
```

```
preserve
clear
loc cat year
import excel "/Users/jorgepena/Desktop/CAMBRIDGE/GDP_DEMP.xlsx", sheet ("Hoja3")
firstrow clear
        graph bar (mean) ag_rsr av_rsr alloc, over (`cat', label (angle (horizontal)
labsize (medium))) ///
                bar (1, fcolor (blue)) bar (2, fcolor (ltblue)) bar (3, fcolor (ltbluish-
gray)) ///
                blabel (bar, orientation (horizontal) format (%9.2f)) ytitle (TFPR (ln)) ///
                legend (order (1 "Aggregate TFP (ln)" 2 "Average TFP (ln)" 3 "Allocative
efficiency")) ///
                graphregion (fcolor (white) lcolor (white) ifcolor (white) ilcolor (white))
                gr display, xsiz (1.5) ysiz (1)
                gr export g.png, replace
                png2rtf using Figures.doc, g (g.png) a
restore
*
preserve
        loc cat ind
        g Y=exp (y)
        bysort `cat': egen SY=sum (Y)
        g sit=Y/SY
        g ag_rsr=sit*rsr
        g x=1
        bysort `cat': egen N=sum (x)
        g av_rsr= (1/N) *rsr
        collapse (sum) ag_rsr av_rsr, by (`cat')
        g alloc=ag_rsr-av_rsr
        graph bar (mean) ag_rsr av_rsr alloc, over (`cat', label (angle (vertical)
labsize (medsmall))) ///
                bar (1, fcolor (blue)) bar (2, fcolor (ltblue)) bar (3, fcolor
(ltbluishgray)) ///
                blabel (bar, orientation (vertical) format (%9.2f)) ytitle (TFPR (ln)) ///
                legend (order (1 "Aggregate TFP (ln)" 2 "Average TFP (ln)" 3 "Allocative
efficiency")) ///
                graphregion (fcolor (white) lcolor (white) ifcolor (white) ilcolor (white))
                gr display, xsiz (1.5) ysiz (1)
                gr export g.png, replace
                png2rtf using Figures.doc, g (g.png) a
restore
*
preserve
        loc cat region
        g Y=exp (y)
        bysort `cat': egen SY=sum (Y)
        g sit=Y/SY
        g ag_rsr=sit*rsr
        g x=1
        bysort `cat': egen N=sum (x)
```

```
        g av_rsr=(1/N)*rsr
        collapse (sum) ag_rsr av_rsr, by(`cat')
        g alloc=ag_rsr-av_rsr
        graph bar (mean) ag_rsr av_rsr alloc, over(`cat', label(angle(vertical)
labsize(medsmall))) ///
                bar(1, fcolor(blue)) bar(2, fcolor(ltblue)) bar(3, fcolor
(ltbluishgray)) ///
                blabel(bar, orientation(vertical) format(%9.2f)) ytitle(TFPR (ln)) ///
                legend(order(1 "Aggregate TFP (ln)" 2 "Average TFP (ln)" 3 "Allocative
efficiency")) ///
                graphregion(fcolor(white) lcolor(white) ifcolor(white) ilcolor(white))
                gr display, xsiz(1.5) ysiz(1)
                gr export g.png, replace
                png2rtf using Figures.doc, g(g.png) a
restore
*
*
*2. Total contribution IC
preserve
        g country=1
        loc cat country
        g Y=exp(y)
        bysort `cat': egen SY=sum(Y)
        g sit=Y/SY
        g x=1
        bysort `cat': egen N=sum(x)
        g nit=(1/N)
        g ag_IC = sit*IC
        g av_IC = nit*IC
        g ag_rsr = sit*rsr
        g av_rsr = nit*rsr
        collapse (sum) ag_rsr av_rsr ag_IC av_IC, by(`cat')
        g cont_ag=100*(ag_IC/ag_rsr)
        g cont_av=100*(av_IC/av_rsr)
        keep cont_ag cont_av
        set obs 2
        replace cont_ag=31.4 in 2
        replace cont_av=32.4 in 2
        g year=2018 in 1
        replace year=2008 in 2
        graph bar (mean) cont_ag cont_av, over(year, label(angle(horizontal) ///
                labsize(medlarge))) bar(1, fcolor(blue)) bar(2, fcolor(ltblue)) ///
                bar(3, fcolor(ltbluishgray)) blabel(bar, size(medium) ///
                orientation(horizontal) format(%9.1f)) ytitle(% Contribution) ///
                legend(order(1 "% Contribution to aggregate tfp" ///
                2 "% Contribution to average tfp") rows(2)) ///
                graphregion(fcolor(white) lcolor(white) ifcolor(white) ilcolor(white))
                gr export g.png, replace
                png2rtf using Figures.doc, g(g.png) a
restore
*
```

```
*
*4. Individual contributions
preserve
    g country=1
    loc cat country
    g Y=exp(y)
    bysort `cat': egen SY=sum(Y)
    g sit=Y/SY
    g x=1
    bysort `cat':egen N=sum(x)
    g nit=(1/N)
    foreach x of varlist `X' `W' {
        g mg_`x'=sit*`x'*_b[`x']
        g me_`x'=nit*`x'*_b[`x']
    }
    g ag_rsr=sit*rsr
    collapse (sum) mg_* me_* ag_rsr, by(`cat')
    foreach x in `X' {
        replace mg_`x'=(mg_`x'/ag_rsr)*100
        replace me_`x'=(me_`x'/ag_rsr)*100
    }
    mkmat mg_*, mat(A)
    mkmat me_*, mat(B)
    mat C=A',B'
    clear
    svmat C
    g cat=_n
    label def cat 1 "Elec. generator" ///
    2 "Crime loss." ///
    3 "Security" ///
    4 "Tax inspections" ///
    5 "Informal comp." ///
    6 "Bribes in taxes" ///
    7 "Equity financing" ///
    8 "Sales after delivery" ///
    9 "Web page use" ///
    10 "Training" ///
    11 "Age"
    label value cat cat
    graph bar (mean) C1 C2, over(cat, label(angle(vertical) labsize(small))) ///
        bar(1, fcolor(blue)) bar(2, fcolor(ltblue)) ///
        bar(3, fcolor(ltbluishgray)) blabel(bar, orientation(vertical) format
(%9.2f)) ///
        ytitle(% Contribution) legend(order(1 "% Contribution to
aggregate tfpIC" ///
        2 "% Contribution to average tfpIC") rows(2)) ///
        graphregion(fcolor(white) lcolor(white) ifcolor(white)
ilcolor(white))
    gr display, xsiz(1.5) ysiz(1)
    gr export g.png, replace
    png2rtf using Figures.doc, g(g.png) a
```

```
restore
*
*
*5. Block contributions
preserve
      g country=1
      loc cat country
      g Y=exp(y)
      bysort `cat' : egen SY=sum(Y)
      g sit=Y/SY
      g x=1
      bysort `cat' : egen N=sum(x)
      g nit=(1/N)
      foreach x of varlist `X' `W' {
             g mg_`x'=sit*`x'*abs(_b[`x'])
             g me_`x'=nit*`x'*abs(_b[`x'])
      }
      g ag_rsr=sit*rsr
      collapse (sum) mg_* me_* ag_rsr, by(`cat')
      foreach x in `X' {
             replace mg_`x'=(mg_`x'/ag_rsr)*100
             replace me_`x'=(me_`x'/ag_rsr)*100
      }
      *
      g A_Inf=mg_av_elecgen
      g
A_Bur=mg_v_crimeloss+mg_av_segur+mg_v_taxinsp+mg_av_infcomp+mg_av_infpaytax
      g A_Fin=mg_v_fxa_equy+mg_v_sales_adl
      g A_Qua=mg_av_internet+mg_av_training
      g A_Oth=mg_v_age
      *
      g B_Inf=me_av_elecgen
      g
B_Bur=me_v_crimeloss+me_av_segur+me_v_taxinsp+me_av_infcomp+me_av_infpaytax
      g B_Fin=me_v_fxa_equy+me_v_sales_adl
      g B_Qua=me_av_internet+me_av_training
      g B_Oth=me_v_age
      *
      keep A_* B_*
      egen A_tot=rsum(A_*)
      egen B_tot=rsum(B_*)
      foreach x in A_Inf A_Bur A_Fin A_Qua A_Oth {
             replace `x'=100*(`x'/A_tot)
      }
      foreach x in B_Inf B_Bur B_Fin B_Qua B_Oth {
             replace `x'=100*(`x'/B_tot)
      }
      drop A_tot B_tot
      mkmat A_*, mat(A)
      mkmat B_*, mat(B)
      mat C=A',B'
```

```
clear
svmat C
g year=2018
set obs 10
replace C1=33.4 in 6
replace C1=36.8 in 7
replace C1=12.4 in 8
replace C1=16.9 in 9
replace C1=0.4 in 10
replace C2=28.3 in 6
replace C2=36.1 in 7
replace C2=11.6 in 8
replace C2=15.9 in 9
replace C2=0.4 in 10
replace year=2008 if year==.
bysort year: g cat=_n
recode cat (1=5) (2=4) (3=3) (4=2) (5=1)
label def cat 5 "Other control vars." ///
4 "Quality, innov. and labor skills" ///
3 "Finance" ///
2 "Red tape, corruption and crime" ///
1 "Infrastructure"
label value cat cat
graph bar (mean) C1 C2, over(year, label(angle(horizontal) labsize
(medsmall))) ///
        over(cat, label(angle(forty_five) labsize(small))) bar(1, fcolor
(blue)) ///
        bar(2, fcolor(ltblue)) bar(3, fcolor(ltbluishgray)) ///
        blabel(bar, size(small) orientation(vertical) format(%9.1f)) ///
        ytitle(% Contribution) legend(order(1 "% Contribution to
aggregate tfpIC" ///
        2 "% Contribution to average tfpIC") rows(2)) graphregion(fcolor
(white) ///
        lcolor(white) ifcolor(white) ilcolor(white))
        gr display, xsiz(1.5) ysiz(1)
        gr export g.png, replace
        png2rtf using Figures.doc, g(g.png) a
restore
*
*
*6. Demeaned/GDP cross-plot
preserve
clear
import excel "/Users/jorgepena/Desktop/CAMBRIDGE/GDP_DEMP.xlsx", sheet("Hoja1")
firstrow clear
twoway (scatter GDPpc Dem if cat==0) (scatter GDPpc Dem if cat==1, mcolor(red) ///
     msize(medium) mlabsize(small) mlabcolor(black) mlabel(mark) mlabsize
(small) ///
     mlabcolor(black)) (scatter GDPpc Dem if cat==2, mcolor(red) msize
(medlarge) ///
```

```
        mlabel(mark) mlabsize(medsmall) mlabcolor(black)) ///
        (lfit GDPpc Dem, lcolor(red)), xline(0, lcolor(black)) yline(0.115, lcolor
(black)) ///
        xtitle("tfpIC") ytitle("GDP per capita") legend(off) ///
        graphregion(fcolor(white) lcolor(white) ifcolor(white) ilcolor(white))
        gr display, xsiz(1.5) ysiz(1)
        gr export g.png, replace
        png2rtf using Figures.doc, g(g.png) a
restore
*
*
*7. Demeaned by country
preserve
clear
import excel "/Users/jorgepena/Desktop/CAMBRIDGE/GDP_DEMP.xlsx", sheet("Hoja2")
firstrow clear
graph bar (mean) Aggregate Average, over(Country, sort(Aggregate) ///
        label(angle(forty_five) labsize(medium))) bar(1, fcolor(blue)) ///
        bar(2, fcolor(ltblue)) bar(3, fcolor(ltbluishgray)) ///
        blabel(bar, size(small) position(outside) orientation(vertical) ///
        format(%9.2f)) ytitle("tfpIC") ///
        legend(order(1 "Aggregate tfpIC" 2 "Average tfpIC") rows(2)) ///
        graphregion(fcolor(white) lcolor(white) ifcolor(white) ilcolor(white))
        gr display, xsiz(1.5) ysiz(1)
        gr export g.png, replace
        png2rtf using Figures.doc, g(g.png) a
restore
*
*
*8. Contributions in 2008
preserve
        import excel "/Users/jorgepena/Desktop/CAMBRIDGE/CONTS_2008.xlsx",
sheet("Hoja1") firstrow clear
        g cat=_n
        label def cat 1 "Days to clear customs to imports" ///
        2 "Average duration of power outages" ///
        3 "Delay to obtain a phone connection" ///
        4 "Losses due to criminal activity" ///
        5 "Illegal payments for protection" ///
        6 "Manager's time spent in bur. Issues" ///
        7 "Sales declared to taxes" ///
        8 "Dummy for informal competition" ///
        9 "Dummy for lawsuit" ///
        10 "Dummy for external auditory" ///
        11 "Dummy for new technology purchased" ///
        12 "Staff-unskilled workers" ///
        13 "Staff-part time workers" ///
        14 "Weeks of training of skilled workers" ///
        15 "Dummy for e-mail" ///
        16 "Age of the firm" ///
```

```
      17 "Dummy for ownership"
      label value cat cat
      graph bar (asis) Conts, over(cat, label(angle(vertical) labsize(small))) ///
            bar(1, fcolor(blue)) bar(2, fcolor(ltblue)) ///
            bar(3, fcolor(ltbluishgray)) blabel(bar, orientation(vertical) format
(%9.2f)) ///
            ytitle(% Contribution) legend(order(1 "% Contribution to aggregate TFP
(ln)" ///
            2 "% Contribution to average TFP (ln)") rows(2)) ///
            graphregion(fcolor(white) lcolor(white) ifcolor(white) ilcolor(white))
            gr display, xsiz(1.5) ysiz(1)
            gr export g.png, replace
            png2rtf using Figures.doc, g(g.png) a
restore
*
*
*9. Coefficients in 2008
preserve
      import excel "/Users/jorgepena/Desktop/CAMBRIDGE/COEFS_2008.xlsx",
sheet("Hoja1")firstrow clear
      g cat=_n
      label def cat 1 "Days to clear customs to imports" ///
      2 "Average duration of power outages" ///
      3 "Delay to obtain a phone connection" ///
      4 "Losses due to criminal activity" ///
      5 "Illegal payments for protection" ///
      6 "Manager's time spent in bur. Issues" ///
      7 "Sales declared to taxes" ///
      8 "Dummy for informal competition" ///
      9 "Dummy for lawsuit" ///
      10 "Dummy for external auditory" ///
      11 "Dummy for new technology purchased" ///
      12 "Staff-unskilled workers" ///
      13 "Staff-part time workers" ///
      14 "Weeks of training of skilled workers" ///
      15 "Dummy for e-mail" ///
      16 "Age of the firm" ///
      17 "Dummy for ownership"
      label value cat cat
      graph bar (asis) Coef, over(cat, label(angle(vertical) labsize(small))) ///
            bar(1, fcolor(blue)) bar(2, fcolor(ltblue)) ///
            bar(3, fcolor(ltbluishgray)) blabel(bar, orientation(vertical) format
(%9.2f)) ///
            ytitle(Value) legend(order(1 "% Contribution to aggregate TFP (ln)" ///
            2 "% Contribution to average TFP (ln)") rows(2)) ///
            graphregion(fcolor(white) lcolor(white) ifcolor(white) ilcolor(white))
            gr display, xsiz(1.5) ysiz(1)
            gr export g.png, replace
            png2rtf using Figures.doc, g(g.png) a
restore
```

References

Ackerberg, D., C. Benkard, S. Berry and Pakes, A. (2007). "Econometric Tools for Analyzing Market Outcomes." In J. J. Heckman and E. E. Leamer (ed.), *Handbook of Econometrics*, 1st ed., vol. 6, chapter 63. Elsevier, 4171–4276.

Ackerberg, D., K. Caves and G. Frazer (2015). "Identification Properties of Recent Production Function Estimators." *Econométrica*, 83(6), 2411–2451.

Ahn, S. (2001). "Firm Dynamics and Productivity Growth: A Review of Micro Evidence From OECD Countries." OECD Economic Department Working Papers 297.

Alexander, W. R. J., J. D. Bell and S. Knowles, (2004). "Quantifying Compliance Costs of Small Businesses in New Zealand." Discussion paper, University of Otago. www.business.otago.ac.nz/econ/research/discussionpapers/DPO406.pdf.

Arellano M. and S. Bond (1991). "Some Test of Specification for Panel Data: Monte Carlo Evidence and Application to Employment Equations." *The Review of Economics Studies*, 58, 277–297.

Aza, C. (2017): Análisis de productividad y medición de la PTF por rama de actividad de la economía española (1995–2007): relación con las TIC y otros determinantes. [translation: Analysis of productivity and measurement of TFP by branch of activity of the Spanish economy (1995–2007): relationship with ICT and other determinants.] PhD thesis, UAM, Spain.

Aza, C. and A. Escribano (2019a). "Efectos de la digitalización y la productividad en la economía Española: Una comparación Internacional." [translation: Effects of digitization and productivity on the Spanish economy: An international comparison]. *UC3M Working Paper* 2019-06.

Aza, C. and A. Escribano (2019b). "Transporte, infraestructura y crecimiento económico en España." [translation: Transport, infraestructures and economic growth in Spain]. *UC3M Working Paper* 2019-18

Barro, R. J. and X. Sala-i-Martin (2004). *Economic Growth*, 2nd ed. Cambridge, MA: The MIT Press

Bartelsman E. J. and M. Doms (2000). "Understanding Productivity: Lessons from Longitudinal Microdata." *Journal of Economic Literature*, 38(3), 569–594.

Bernard, A. B, J. Eaton, J. B. Jensen and S. Kortum (2003). "Plants and Productivity in International Trade." *American Economic Review*, 93(4), 1268–1290.

Blundell R. and S. Bond (1998). "Initial Conditions and Moment Restrictions in Dynamic Panel Data Models." *Journal of Econometrics*, 87, 115–143.

Blundell R. and S. Bond (2000). "GMM Estimation with Persistent Panel Data: An Application to Production Functions." *Econometric Reviews*, 19(3), 321–340.

Bosworth, B. and S. Collins (2003). "The Empirics of Growth: An Update." The Brookings Institution. Washington, DC. Processed.

Brunel, S. (2004) "L'Afrique: Un Continent en Réserve de Développement," *Editions Bréal*, Rosny-sous-Bois.

Chamberlain G. (1982). "Multivariate Regressions Models for Panel Data." *Journal of Econometrics* 18.

Cohen, W. and D. Levinthal (1989). "Innovation and Learning: The Two Faces of R&D." *Economic Journal* 99, 569–596.

Cohen, W. and D. Levinthal (1990). "Absorptive Capacity: A New Perspective on Learning and Innovation." *Administrative Science Quarterly* 35(1), 128–152.

Cole, H. L., L. E. Ohanian, A. Riascos and J. A. Schmitz Jr. (2004). "Latin America in the Rearview Mirror." National Bureau of Economic Research WP #11008, December.

Cusolito, A. P., D. Lederman and J. Pena (2020). "The Effects of Digital-Technology Adoption on Productivity and Factor Demand: Firm-Level Evidence from Developing Countries." *Policy Research Working Paper; No. 9333*. World Bank, Washington, DC. https://openknowledge.worldbank.org /handle/10986/34251 License: CC BY 3.0 IGO.

de Loecker, J. (2013). "Detecting Learning by Exporting." *American Economic Journal: Microeconomics*, 5(3), 1–21.

de Orte M. (2010). Economic Determinants of India's Investment Climate. Ph.D. Dissertation UNED.

de Soto, Hernando (2002). *The Mystery of Capital: Why Capitalism Triumphs in the West and Fails Everywhere Else*. New York: Basic Books Press.

Debreu, G. (1951), "The Coefficient of Resource Utilization," *Econometrica* 19, 273–292.

Denison, E. F. (1962). The sources of economic growth in the united States and the alternative before us. Supplementary paper 13, Committee for Economic Development.

Denison, E. F. (1974). *Accounting for United States Economic Growth 1929–1969*. Washington DC: The Brookings Institution.

Dethier J. J., M. Hirn and S. Straub (2008). "Explaining enterprise performance in developing countries with business climate survey data." *The World Bank Policy Research Working Paper #4792*.

Diewert W. E. and A. O. Nakamura (2003) "The Measurement of Aggregate Total Factor Productivity Growth." In J. J. Heckman and E. E. Leamer (eds.). *Handbook of Econometrics*, Vol. 6. Chicago: North Holland, 127–159.

Dollar, D., M. Hallward-Driemeier and T. Mengistae (2003). "Investment Climate and Firm Performance in Developing Economies." Washington, DC, World Bank.

Dollar, D., A. Shi, S. Wang and L. C. Xu (2004). "Improving City Competitiveness through the Investment Climate: Ranking 23 Chinese Cities." Washington, DC, World Bank.

Dollar, D., M. Hallward-Driemeier and T. Mengistae (2004). "Investment Climate and International Integration." Washington, DC, World Bank.

Dollar, D., M. Hallward-Driemeier and T. Mengistae, (2005). "Investment Climate and Firm Performance in Developing Economies." Economic Development and Cultural Change, 54, 1–31. http://doi.org/10.1086/431262.

Escribano, A., A. Fosfuri and J. Tribo (2009). "Managing Knowledge Spillovers: The Impact of Absorptive Capacity on Innovation Performance." *Research Policy. Volume* 38, 96–105.

Escribano, A. and J. L. Guasch (2004). "Econometric Methodology for Investment Climate Assessments (ICA) on Productivity using Firm Level Data: The Case of Guatemala, Honduras and Nicaragua." Mimeo World Bank, June.

Escribano, A. and J. L. Guasch (2005). "Assessing the Impact of the Investment Climate on Productivity using Firm Level Data: Methodology and the Cases of Guatemala, Honduras and Nicaragua." *Policy Research Working Paper #* 3621, The World Bank, June.

Escribano, A., J. L. Guasch and J. Pena (2010): "Assessing the impact of infrastructure quality on firm productivity in Africa: Cross-country comparisons based on investment climate surveys from 1999 to 2005." *Policy Research Working Paper Series 5191*, The World Bank.

Escribano A., J. L. Guasch and J. Pena (2019). "Investment Climate Effects on Alternative Productivity Measures." *Working Paper 19–09*, Universidad Carlos III de Madrid.

Escribano, A., J. L. Guasch, M. de Orte and J. Pena (2008a): "Investment Climate Assessment Based on Demean Olley and Pakes Decompositions: Methodology and Applications to Turkey's Investment Climate Survey," *Working Paper # 08–20 (12)*, Universidad Carlos III de Madrid, Spain.

Escribano, A., J. L. Guasch, M. de Orte, and J. Pena (2008b): "Investment Climate and Firm's Economic Performance: Econometric Methodology and Application to Turkey's Investment Climate Survey" *Working Paper #* 08–21 (13), Universidad Carlos III de Madrid, Spain.

Escribano, A., J. L. Guasch, M. de Orte and J. Pena (2009): "Investment Climate Assessment in Indonesia, Malaysia, Philippines and Thailand:

Results from Pooling Firm Level Data." Special Issue on the Econometric Analysis of Panel Data, *Singapore Economic Review*, 54(3), 335–366.

Booribano A. and R. Stucchi (2013). "Does Recession Drive Convergence in Firms' Productivity? Evidence from Spanish Manufacturing Firms." Joint with Rodolfo Stucchi. *Journal of Productivity Analysis*, 41, 339–349.

Escribano, A. and G. Sucarrat (2012). "Automated model selection in finance: General-to-specific modeling of the mean and volatility specifications." *Oxford Bulletin of Economics and Statistics*, 74(5), 716–735.

Estache, A. (2005). "What Do We Know About Sub-Saharan Africa's Infrastructure and the Impact of Its 1990 Reforms?" Mimeo, World Bank, Washington, DC.

EU KLEMS (2017). EU KLEMS Growth and Productivity Accounts, www .euklems.net

EU KLEMS (2018). World KLEMS Growth and Productivity Accounts, www .euklems.net

Fajnzylber P., J. L. Guasch and J. H. López (2009). *Does Investment Climate Matter? Microeconomic Foundations of Growth in Latin America*. Washington, DC: The World Bank.

Farrell, M. (1957), "The Measurement of Productive Efficiency," *Journal of the Royal Statistical Society A, General*, 120, 253–281.

Ferrari A. and I. S. Dhingra (2009). *India's Investment Climate: Voices of Indian Business*. Washington, DC: The World Bank.

Foster L., J. Haltiwanger and C. J. Krizan (1998). "Aggregate Productivity Growth: Lessons from Microeconomic Evidence." *NBER Working Paper* W6803.

Foster, L., J. Haltiwanger, and C. Syverson (2008). "Reallocation, Firm Turnover, and Efficiency: Selection on Productivity or Profitability?" American Economic Review, 98(1), 394–425.

Fried, H. O., C. A. Knox-Lovell, and S. S. Schmidt (ed.). (2008). *The Measurement of Productive Efficiency and Productivity Growth*. Oxford: Oxford University Press.

Green, W. H. (2008). The econometric approach to efficiency analysis. In H. O. Fried C.A. Knox Lovell and S. S. Schmidt, (ed.). *The Measurement of Productive Efficiency and Productivity Growth*. Oxford: Oxford University Press 92–250.

Grifell-Tatjé, E. and C. A. Knox-Lovell (2015). Productivity Accounting: The Economic of Business Performance. Cambridge: Cambridge University Press.

Griliches, Z. (1996). "The Discovery of the Residual: A Historical Note." *Journal of Economic Literature*, 34, 1324–1330.

Griliches, Z. and J. Mairesse (1997). "Production Functions: The Search for Identification." In S. Strom (ed.) *Essays in Honor of Ragnar Frisch,*

Econometric Society Monograph Series. Cambridge: Cambridge University Press, 95–123.

Hall, R. E. (1990). "Invariance Properties of Solow's Productivity Residual." In P. Diamond (ed.). *Growth, Productivity, Employment.* Cambridge: MIT Press, 1–53.

Hall, R. E. and C.I. Jones (1999). "Why Do Some Countries So Much More Output per Worker than Others?" *The Quarterly Journal of Economics,* 114 (1), 83–116.

Haltiwanger, J. (2002). "Understanding Economic Growth: The Need for Micro Evidence." *New Zealand Economic Papers* 36(1), 33–58.

Haltiwanger, J. (2016). "Firm Dynamics and Productivity: TFPQ, TFPR, and Demand Side Factors." *Economic Journal, The Latin American and Caribbean Economic Association – LACEA,* 0(Fall 2016), 3–26.

Hendry, D. F. and H. M. Krolzig (2001). *Automatic Econometric Model Selection.* London: Timberlake Consultants Press.

Hendry, D. F. and H.M. Krolzig (2005). "The Properties of Automatic GETS Modeling." *Economic Journal,* 115, C32–C61.

Hendry, D. F. and B. Nielsen (2007). *Econometric Modeling: A Likelihood Approach.* Princeton: Princeton University Press.

Hidalgo-Cabrillana, A. and A. Eros (2008). "On Finance as a Theory of TFP, Cross-Industry Productivity Differences, and Economic Rents." *International Economic Review* 49(2), 437–473.

Hoover, K. D. and S. J. Perez (1999). "Data Mining Reconsidered: Encompassing and the General-to-Specific Approach to Specification Search. *Econometrics Journal,* 2, 167–191.

Hsieh, C. and P. Klenow (2009). "Misallocation and Manufacturing TFP in China and India." The Quarterly Journal of Economics, 124(4), 1403–1448.

Hulten, Ch. R. (2001). "Total Factor Productivity: A Short Biography." In Ch. R. Hulten, E. R. Dean and M. J. Harper (eds.). *New Developments in Productivity Analysis.* Chicago: The University of Chicago Press, 1–47.

Jorgenson, D. W. (2001). "Information Technology and the U.S. Economy," *The American Economic Review,* 91(1), 1–32.

Jorgenson, D. W., F. Gollop and B. Fraumeni (1987). *Productivity and U.S. Economic Growth.* Cambridge: Harvard University Press.

Jorgenson D. W. and Z. Griliches (1967). "The Explanation of Productivity Change." *Review of Economic Studies,* 34(3), 249–283.

Jorgenson, D. W., M. S. Ho and K. J. Stiroh (2005): "Growth of U.S. Industries and Investments in Information Technology and Higher Education" NBER Chapters, in: Measuring Capital in the New Economy, pp. 403–478, National Bureau of Economic Research, Inc. (pp. 403–478).

Katayama, H., S. Lu and J. R. Tybout (2009). "Firm-Level Productivity Studies: Illusions and a solution." *International Journal of Industrial Organization*, 27(3), 403–413.

Kasper, W. (2002), "Losing Sight of the Lodestar of Economic Freedom: A Report Card on New Zealand's Economic Reform," NZ Business Roundtable.

Kerr, R. (2002). "The Quagmire of Regulation," NZ Business Roundtable. www.nzbr.org.nz/documents/speeches/speeches-200/the_quagmire_of_regu lation.pdf.

Levinsohn, J. and M. J. Melitz (2001). "Productivity in a Differentiated Products Market Equilibrium." Mimeo.

Levinsohn J. and A. Petrin (2003). "Estimating Production Functions Using Inputs to Control for Unobservables." *Review of Economic Studies*, 70, 317–341.

Marschak, J. and W. H. Andrews (1944). "Random Simultaneous Equations and the Theory of Production." *Econometrica*, 12 (3,4), 143–205.

Mas, M. and J. C. Robledo (2010): "Productividad: una perspectiva internacional y sectorial." *Fundación BBVA*.

McMillan, J. (1998). "Managing Economic Change: Lessons from New Zeland", *The World Economy*, *21*, 827–43.

McMillan, J. (2004). "A Flexible Economy? Entrepreneurship and Productivity in New Zealand", Working Paper, Graduate Scholl of Business, Stanford University, Stanford, CA.

Melitz, M. (2003). "The Impact of Trade on Intra-Industry Reallocations and Aggregate Industry Productivity," *Econometrica*, 71(6), 1695–1725

OECD (2001a). OECD Manual: "Measuring Productivity, Measurement of Aggregate and Industry-Level Productivity Growth." Paris: OECD.

OECD (2001b). Businesses' Views on Red Tape. Paris: OECD. www1.oecd.org /publications/e-book/4201101E.PDF.

Olley, G. S. and A. Pakes (1996). "The Dynamics of Productivity in the Telecommunications Equipment Industry." *Econometrica*, 64(6), 1263–1297.

Pena, J. (2009). Essays on the Investment Climate and Its Effects on Firm's Efficiency. Ph.D. Dissertation. UNED.

Pena, J. and A. Escribano (2021). "Missing Values: An Econometric Approach." Working Paper, Universidad Carlos III de Madrid.

Pérez, F. and Benages, E 2017. "The Role of Capital Accumulation in the Evolution of Total Factor Productivity in Spain," *International Productivity Monitor, Centre for the Study of Living Standards*, 33, 24–50.

Perry, G. E., W. F. Maloney, O. S. Arias, P. Fajnzylber, A. D. Mason and J. Saavedra-Chanduvi (2007). *Informality: Exit and Exclusion*. Washington, DC: The World Bank.

Prescott, E. C. (1998) "Needed: A Theory of Total Factor Productivity." *International Economic Review*, 39, 525–552.

Raghunathan, T. E., J. Lepkowski, J. Van Hoewyk and P. Solenberger (2001). "A Multivariate Technique for Multiply Imputing Missing Values Using a Sequence of Regression Models." *Survey Methodology*, 27(1), 85–95.

Rodrik, D. and A. Subramanian (2004). "From 'Hindu Growth to Productivity Surge: The Mystery of the Indian Growth Transition." Harvard University, Cambridge, MA. Processed.

Solow, R. M. (1957). "Technical Change and the Aggregate Production Function" *The Review of Economics and Statistics*, 39(3), 312–320.

Timmer, M. P., R. Inklaar, M. O'Mahony and B. van Ark (2010). *Economic Growth in Europe: A Comparative Industry Perspective*. Cambridge: Cambridge University Press.

Törnqvist, L. (1936). "The Bank of Finland's Consumption Price Index." *Bank of Finland Monthly Bulletin* 10, 1–8.

Van Buuren, V., J. P. L. Brands, C. G. M. Groothuis-Oudshoorn and D. B. Rubin (2006). "Fully conditional specification in multivariate imputation." *Journal of Statistical Computation and Simulation*, 76(12), 1049–1064.

Wilkinson, B. (2001). "Constraining Government Regulation." NZ Business Roundtable. www.nzbr.org.nz/documents/publications/publications-2001/constraining_govt.pdf.

Wooldridge J. M. (2002). *Econometric Analysis of Cross Section and Panel Data*. Cambridge, MA: The MIT Press.

Wooldridge J. M. (2009). "On Estimating Firm-Level Production Functions Using Proxy Variables to Control for Unobservables." *Economics Letters*, 104(3), 112–114.

World Bank 2003. "Doing Business in 2004: Understanding Regulation." Washington, DC: World Bank.

World Bank 2004a. "Doing Business in 2005: Removing Obstacles to Growth." Washington, DC: World Bank.

World Bank 2004b. "2003 Annual Review of Development Effectiveness: The Effectiveness of Bank Support for Policy Reform. Report 28290." Washington, DC: World Bank Operations Evaluation Department.

World Bank 2005. "World Development Report 2005: A Better Investment Climate for Everyone." Washington, DC: World Bank and Oxford University Press.

World Bank (2010a). "Regulatory Governance in Developing Countries." Washington, DC: World Bank. https://openknowledge.worldbank.org/handle/10986/27881 License: CC BY 3.0 IGO

World Bank (2010b). "How to Reform Business Licenses." Washington, DC: World Bank.

World Bank (2011). "How to Reform Business Inspections, Design, Implementation, Challenges." Washington, DC. World Bank

Acknowledgments

This Element extends and updates the econometric methodology initially developed in working papers carried out over the last fifteen years by Escribano and Pena and co-authors, for empirical country assessments of World Bank reports. We are in debted to J. L. Guasch for suggesting we work in the methodology of IC surveys and in fact the first paper was a joint work with him. The objective is to extend and unify the robust empirical productivity methodology that has been used to evaluate the surveys regarding the business situation, investment climate assessment (ICA), of more than forty-two developing and emerging countries. We are indebted to three referees and to D. Ackerberg, J. M. Dufour, J. Levinsohn, A. Pakes and J. Wooldridge for the suggestions given in previous versions of this productivity methodology. We have also benefited from the suggestions of participants in meetings of the American Economic Association, in seminars and courses taught by A. Escribano at the World Bank, Washington, DC (USA) and Vienna (Austria), at CORE (UCL, Belgium) and from participants in the Master's courses given at the University Carlos III of Madrid.

Funding Information

Álvaro Escribano acknowledges the funding from the Spanish Ministry of Economy, Industry and Competitiveness (ECO2015-68715-R, ECO2016-00105–001), Maria de Maeztu Grant (MDM 2014–0431) and Agencia Estatal de Investigación (2019/00419/001).

Cambridge Elements ≡

Economics of Emerging Markets

Bruno S. Sergi
Harvard University

Editor Bruno S. Sergi is an instructor at Harvard University, and an associate of the Harvard University Davis Center for Russian and Eurasian Studies and Harvard Ukrainian Research Institute. He is Academic Series Editor of the Cambridge *Elements in the Economics of Emerging Markets* (Cambridge University Press), a co-editor of the *Lab for Entrepreneurship and Development* book series, and Associate Editor of *The American Economist*. Concurrently, he teaches International Economics at the University of Messina, is Scientific Director of the Lab for Entrepreneurship and Development (LEAD), and a co-founder and Scientific Director of the International Center for Emerging Markets Research at RUDN University in Moscow. He has published over 150 articles in professional journals and twenty-one books as author, co-author, editor and co-editor.

About the Series

The aim of this Elements series is to deliver state-of-the-art, comprehensive coverage of the knowledge developed to date, including the dynamics and prospects of these economies, focusing on emerging markets' economics, finance, banking, technology advances, trade, demographic challenges, and their economic relations with the rest of the world, as well as the causal factors and limits of economic policy in these markets.

Printed in the United States
by Baker & Taylor Publisher Services